Table of Contents

Praise for Jobs Over Fifty

"We all know that the Aging of America is upon us, yet employers have yet to recognize there's a lot of ROI left in older adults. Whether it'spointing out how to level the technology playing field, navigating age bias inthe hiring process or just having a solid plan, this book is a MUST read foranyone 50+ looking for work and a SHOULD read for anyone in a hiringposition." Ed Rose, Founder and CEO, Serality.

"A great guide for those over fifty faced with an unexpected career change. Straightforward pragmatic advice offered with humor by a well-respected executive who has proven himself to be both highly resilient and a man with integrity." Ann Leyva, Senior Vice President of Human Resources, David's Bridal.

"Great guide for those of us over fifty that are looking for their next great career opportunity. Well written and easy to follow." Craig Debenham, Vice President of Stores, Torrid.

"This inexpensive kindle book is full of practical advise and wisdom from someone who has experienced the job search after 50. It is both strategic and tactical and addresses critical post recession concerns for post 50 workers!" John Fontana, President, Woodstock Theological Institute.

Chapter One: Reality

My forty-something boss wanted me out. He started by regaling me with stories of what the CFO of IBM was getting done in his job. At that time, IBM was one of our largest and most important clients. I started to respond that the IBM CFO made about fifty times what I did, and *he* was supported by his *talented* boss, but I thought better of it. In any case, I realized that it was time to find something new. I launched a full-scale action and, after a few months, landed a new CFO slot.

It was great for a while; I reported to a very experienced mid-fifties executive. We were on our way to being a great team. However, as a result of an acquisition, I found myself reporting to another forty -something, headstrong CEO. Having significant experience as CFO, I had a strong view of what needed to be done in the finance and accounting realm in our fast-growing technology company. However, as the technology euphoria of 1999 and 2000 was replaced by the technology depression of 2001, my relationship with the CEO deteriorated. Soon, I was out, replaced by a mid-thirties CFO, who had no experience in technology companies.

The youth movement there was well underway.

This time finding a new position became more of a pitched battle. I was old, over-the-hill. Companies want youth and vigor, not experience and savvy.

There it is–the new reality.

I was over fifty. A dinosaur. Ready to be put out to pasture. Washed up.

That is all too often the view of the marketplace. Recently, a search firm called me and described an outstanding CFO opportunity. Great pay, in a city I considered a desirable place to live, for a company that was the industry leader in its field. My experience was a great match. I knew I was a great candidate. However, after some discussions, all of sudden I was told my qualifications fell short. The search firm and the client had concluded that I didn't have enough experience dealing with Boards of Directors. I responded by summarizing my extensive qualifications in that regard, but the recruiter's mind was made up. I would not be presented as a candidate.

I was more than disappointed. After months of looking, this was clearly the best opportunity, and the best fit, that I had seen. I was confident that if I could meet the CEO, I would get the job. But I wasn't going to get to meet the CEO; my board experience was too light. However, I have extensive experience at the board level, so something did not ring true. A little detective work told the real tale: the new CEO was forty years old; the incumbent CFO who was on his way out was my age. A youth movement at that company was underway.

As I looked around, the reality of the new generational war was everywhere. The company that pushed me out replaced me with a 35 year old. A multi-billion company in my home town doing business throughout the U.S. hired a 30 year old CFO. I had known it, heard about it, but now it was my turn to experience it.[1] Discrimination was rampant–I wasn't being considered for positions simply due to no factor other than my age. I joined a local networking group. (This is an excellent idea which we'll talk much more about later). It became obvious that the under- forty year old members of the group were finding new positions far faster than the over -fifties.

In summary, here is the issue: are you going to learn to say "Welcome to Wal-Mart", join the legions saying "Would you like fries with that?" or are you going to fight back and win the job that your hard-earned business battle scars have prepared you for?

Eventually I landed a position with a total annual compensation well into six figures. My lessons are in this book.

Remember, you may be a dinosaur, but *dinosaurs ruled the earth for about 165 million years....*

Chapter 2 Self-Assessment

Are you ready to compete with the best-qualified 35 year-old in America for your next job?

That's what you are up against.

Our formula is simple: you must be capable of using current technology proficiently, you must be serious about health and fitness and your appearance must reflect vigor and eagerness to perform. Then you must exploit the advantage of your superior experience.

It is time for an honest self-assessment.

How good are you at using current technology? Are you in shape? What would happen if you had to go back to the dating circuit?

Think through these statements:

1. My LinkedIn page is, well, dynamite. I've attended webinars on LinkedIn and taken the advice to create a world-class representation of my skills and capabilities.
2. I'm as close to a household name on Twitter as you can find.
3. My line of work requires the use of a standard set of software tools and I'm very adept.
4. Other workers come to me to learn how to take advantage of advanced software features.
5. I have my own website, and, if I must say so, it's pretty cool.
6. I was one of the first users of smart phones. I use more apps than Tim Cook.
7. I text faster than most people can talk.

Do you strongly agree with those?

How about these:

1. Honestly, I'm in the best shape of my life.
2. I'm on a really good, challenging fitness routine.
3. I'm in way better shape than most people my age.

4. OK, I don't like it, but I'm (in the gym) (swimming laps in the pool)
    (jogging three miles) (at the yoga studio) at least five times a week.
5. If I lost five pounds, I would weigh what I did when I graduate from
    high school.

And finally these:

1. While I'm not a kid, I know what is in fashion, and I dress
    appropriately for my age.
2. I take good care of myself; my teeth are bright white, my hair style is
    current, and I take care of body hair like an Olympic swimmer.

Now, one other very important area. People will discuss almost anything
other than their personal financial situation. But you must be brutally honest
with yourself: how long can you go without a paycheck? That has clear,
direct implications for your search for a new position. If you are financially
independent, you can await the perfect job. If you are rapidly running out of
money, you may have to accept a less than desirable position to keep a roof
over your head. We have a few financial points later that might help. But
don't dodge this question; if you need to start a new job in thirty days, you'll
have to modify our program, and work extreme hours to make it happen.

Chapter 3 Abstract

"We must make this campaign an exceedingly active one. Only thus can a weaker country cope with a stronger. It must make up in activity what it lacks in strength." General Thomas "Stonewall" Jackson.

In this brief chapter, we outline the program you are going to undertake as you use this book as a tool to find your next position.

Many of these activities are going to occur simultaneously, requiring you to manage your daily calendar judiciously (I provide strong direction on that topic as well).

The themes of this book are straightforward:

- Take a series of actions to reduce the risk that you won't be considered for a position because of your age.
- Develop powerful marketing messages that emphasize your experience and that position you favorably versus younger candidates.
- Use the strength and ubiquity of the Internet to distribute those marketing messages to thousands of contacts.
- Customize your marketing materials specifically for targeted opportunities.
- Prepare you to be sensationally effective in every type of meeting and interview.

If you are newly out of work, or if you know (or even strongly suspect) that you will lose your job soon, say, thirty days after a merger or after a large contract is completed, then I recommend you follow the process outlined in this book in detail. If you do, it will probably be thirty days before you actually contact any potential employers or schedule any of the myriad personal contact efforts you are going to undertake, such as attending network meetings or responding to online job ads.

If you have been out of work for a while and you are just now starting to use this book, you may find this approach harder because you:

- May be having some success using another approach (even though you haven't landed a position);
- (Unfortunately like me) have previous experience in finding another

position, and have been relying on the techniques that worked for you
in the past;
- Have outplacement and are following their structured program;
- Have tried some other approaches which aren't working, so that your
search has no momentum,
- Feel pressure from family, your financial situation, or just your ego,
to find a job and get back to work – any work.

If you are a member of this group, I recommend that you scan a few chapters
to see if you are ready to change from your current techniques to this one.
You don't have much to lose by reviewing the book – I'll be surprised if you
don't pick up a few pointers of value. If you find this approach makes sense,
then go back to chapter four and work your way through.

Let's get started

Chapter 4 Basic Training

"If in training soldiers, commands are habitually enforced, the army will be well-disciplined." Sun Tzu, <u>The Art of War</u>.

You've got a lot to do.

You are going to manage marketing, health, fitness and appearance programs simultaneously. Many people that you were counting on are going to disappear like the townsfolk Gary Cooper tried to enlist to help him in *High Noon*.

The US Army has recognized something very important. As soldiers became physically larger, quicker and stronger, constantly connected with GPS, armed with amazing personal firepower, with real-time audio and video linkage, and night vision capability, a sea change in the foot soldier has occurred. The Army is witnessing the return of the medieval knight or the samurai. The ultimate fighting force is an individual soldier–but connected to an awesome network. This realization was aptly captured in the advertising slogan of "An Army of One".

You too must become an Army of One. And you too must connect to a powerful network.

Let's get physical. The harsh reality of America today is that youth is worshipped and age is discriminated against. And, fat people are further discriminated against. For you to land the next job, you should appear as active and physically fit as possible. You must look as young is possible. And you've got to employ every trick to offset your age handicap.

The objective: the lean and hungry look. Shakespeare was a great observer, and his line from *Julius Caesar* "yon Cassius has that lean and hungry look", while written centuries ago, remains equally true today: thin and fit bespeaks self-discipline, good health and the capability to work long and hard. Obviously these are attractive characteristics in any job candidate. For the woman reader, I must say in truth that I think this is even more important for you than a man.

If you aren't currently in great shape, you need to find your ideal weight and set a goal to get there as part of this job changing plan.(There are a number of online sources for researching your ideal weight including Web MD (www.webmd.com) and Weight Watchers (www.weightwatchers.com). If you are already lean as a whippet, and on a great exercise plan, you can skip this section up to the "General Appearance" section, which follows the Exercise section. I'm not going to cover fitness programs here-that genre is well covered indeed. But you and I already know the essence of all fitness programs: eat less, eat smarter, and exercise more. If you are not in a regular program, start now. I feel strongly about this; there are a multitude of benefits from exercising; helping you to find a new position is probably the least important one. This is why this topic is covered early in the book, not towards the end. If you are not in shape, you need to start NOW, because it is going to take a while to produce the desired results.

You need a two-part exercise program: an aerobic program to reduce weight and tune your most important muscle – your heart; and a weight-training program to improve your appearance. As an important additional benefit, there is a lot of evidence that improved physical condition also improves mental acuity. That will be critical in your job competition against youngsters.

Are you a member of a gym? If you are, get in the habit of going every day and getting into a serious routine. Other members who are serious in their workouts will notice, by working out with them you can create a positive, self-reinforcing cycle. If your membership includes some kind of individual coaching and training, you should certainly take advantage of it.

I searched the Internet looking for good sites to help with exercise. There are hundreds of thousands, maybe millions. I found a few that don't require one to sign up for anything but have some interesting exercise regimes and challenging programs. The first is Oprah Winfrey's site: www.oprah.com . As I write this, the home page features "Dr. Oz 20 minute workout". A second is *Shape* magazine's www.shape.com . Click on the "Fitness" tab for an excellent variety of workout and training programs. And guys, just because these are female-oriented sites, don't think there aren't some very tough, demanding routines. Men's Health magazine has good ideas in every issue, but, frankly, the web site is a mess. My final exercise site is Runner's

World magazine: (www.runnersworld.com), where you'll find tips on running (obviously) but also cross-training, running and strength training, etc. Another site with some good tips: http://www.acefitness.org/.

And the development of programs for your smartphone and dedicated devices like fitbit provide another vehicle for finding fitness routines, tracking and improving performance.

Play around with these and develop your own program. Remember the adage you always hear: if you aren't exercising regularly currently, don't begin a program without consulting a physician. Take your time to build up. Forget the stuff about playing through the pain: at our age, pains are important messages that should be heeded. If it hurts, stop.

General appearance

Now that your exercise program is underway, there are a number of other actions we can take to improve appearance. When fired by my forty-something boss, and knowing the degree of difficulty I was about to face, in addition to stepping up my exercise program, I went to my dentist for a tooth whitening. It was painless, and did indeed brighten my smile. With a little less paunch and a whiter smile, I looked better and felt more confident.

While I haven't yet had any cosmetic surgery, I am not opposed to it, and probably will have some done one day.

Take a hard look at yourself in the mirror. Personally, I wouldn't consider any body surgeries until my exercise program is well underway and getting results. Then I would decide whether to move forward with tummy tuck, liposuction, a face lift or anything more exotic. If you conclude that is appropriate for you and you can afford it without harming your financial condition, my view is go for it. If you've been thinking about having some crows' feet tightened up, or something else done facially, find the best doctor in that field, and get her advice. But remember, losing that fat and getting toned up is the first priority.

A friend of mine had hair transplantation, and I think it looks great. While I didn't think his hair looked that bad prior to the surgery, he did, and in his field youthful appearance is critical. He feels better, more confident, and began getting more work immediately.

I discussed cosmetic surgery with a very successful executive recruiter over lunch. She agreed that the time might come that she would have some cosmetic work, but she hadn't had any yet. She further agreed that appearance was an important factor in being presented as a candidate, or as an executive recruiter attempting to win an employer mandate. Then, after we finished our salads and began the main course, she mentioned that she *had* done *"a little"* done work on her eyelids. Finally, during after-dinner coffee, she added that she had some small liposuction done…. I still wonder what other little procedures she failed to mention. I personally know senior executives that have had cosmetic work done from dental implants creating the perfect smile, to eyelid tightening, breast implants to major cosmetic surgery. Don't rule cosmetic surgery out too quickly. (I'll repeat the caveat: this needs to be something you can afford without pressuring your budget).

And one last warning: if you run an Internet search for Cosmetic Surgery Gone Wrong, you'll see a lot of very spooky stuff. When I ran that search there were 928,000 items. Do your homework and think twice. There's nothing wrong with aging gracefully, I actually prefer seeing people who are OK with some laugh lines.

<u>Yes, You Really Do Have to Dress For Success</u>

<u>The Dress Uniform</u>

One advantage of experience is that you should know how to present yourself. But let's just review: one should always dress conservatively when meeting anyone related to finding your next position. Whether it is an informal networking meeting, an interview with a recruiter, or an interview with a company, dress a touch more conservatively than might be expected. Meeting someone at Starbucks? Even if you think they are coming in jeans, wear a sport coat or nice pants suit. For almost any other meeting, business dresses and suits and ties are mandatory. Shoes, of course, are dress –up and men's shoes absolutely must be shined.

Unfortunately, we live in a time when many grew up without an education on how to dress professionally. I've seen some shocking examples lately, including a young sales executive calling on my company who had neglected to cut the brand label off of the sleeve of his suit coat. And I was just attended a wedding where a teenager showed up in some kind camp shirt with flames on it, shorts, beat-up basketball shoes and a cap which he wore sideways. I can only blame his parents.

So here are some basics. For guys: Match your socks to your shoes. Black shoes, black socks. If you are wearing a charcoal gray suit, I'll let you wear some very dark gray socks. A little shirt cuff should show – but just a little – a quarter inch – up to maybe three quarters of an inch if you are wearing French cuffs and cufflinks. Any longer – you look like you don't know how to buy a shirt, or a suit, or both. No cuff showing is almost as bad – particularly if the coat sleeves are half-way across your hands. For gals: a dress with heels or a dressy slacks and top outfit. (Dresses are no longer required).

With a suit, wear a straight or European collar shirt – not a button down shirt. Make sure the collar stays (sometimes called "collar stiffeners") are in the collar – nothing looks worse than one side of a collar soaring 45 degrees up.

Recently I was watching CNBC (if you are looking for a position in private industry I recommend that you watch this or Bloomberg Television to stay on top of business and economic developments). As is frequently the case, CNBC was switching from one "expert" to another "expert". One had a nice spread collar shirt, lovely tie and professional-looking suit. The other had forgotten a collar stay and had a shirt collar sticking straight up like a flagpole. It was so incredibly distracting that I found it difficult to concentrate on the message. He still appears regularly on business television and I remember his flying shirt collar every time.

During the tech bubble "business casual" became the standard. While in some cities and industries that remains, I've noticed that the New York City crowd has gone back to coat, tie, dresses and heels. We'll spend more time on this in Chapter 20.

Personal Grooming

Lastly, things a drill sergeant will tell you, your mother might tell you, but probably no one else will: As you age, you get hair in all kinds of unattractive places.

You are not going to a networking meeting, much less an interview, with hair in inappropriate places ever again.

Guys: old men get ear hair. Years ago, old-fashioned real barbers clipped ear hair when doing a regular haircut-your grandfather never had visible ear hair. Stylists don't. For some reason, many men seem oblivious to the fact that their ears are taking on primate qualities. A few years ago, I was privileged to attend the board meetings of a consumer electronics company. On the board was one of Dallas' preeminent lawyers. This brilliant attorney and litigator was a masthead partner for a major law firm. He had made a sizeable personal fortune, dressed impeccably, but had more hair coming out of his ears than Chewbacca. I wanted to get in there with an industrial hedge trimmer. Perhaps someone will read this book, recognize him and drop him an anonymous note to see this page.

There are many devices to trim that stuff. Do it regularly.

Gals: lip hair went out with your grandmother. I don't care how much it hurts to get it waxed. It has got to go.

Gals: This isn't France. Shave your legs & under your arms.

Both: nose hair is disgusting. It will get you disqualified from every job. No one wants to ever see your nose hair. Deal with it.

Finally men, many of you reading this book are old enough to remember Senator Sam Ervin. He is remembered for his outstanding work on the Watergate Committee, and also for his bushy eyebrows. Since you aren't a senator, you can't get away with porcupine-quill eyebrows (much less a mono-brow). Trim them back; pluck them, whatever it takes to get them looking good. I must confess that I deal with this every day. I wish I could grow hair on the top of my head like I can grow eyebrows.

Both men and women: network news anchors are good guides to stylish but conservative business apparel, current hairstyles and so on. Watch the network evening news for a few days to see what the pros are wearing.

(I'll remind you again in the 24 hour countdown).

Before any meeting, find a restroom and make sure that hair, lipstick, makeup, and tie are perfect. No food between your teeth and no lipstick on your teeth.

Insider's tip. If you haven't visited offices (including search firms) in New York, L.A or Chicago, some extra time is required. First, traffic in both places is unpredictable; give yourself a time cushion. Second, expect building security and a bag search. Third, expect that restrooms won't be available to the general public. You'll have to get to the office, see the receptionist, get a key, check yourself out and return. Build time for all that in your schedule – and, as your parents always told you, go before you leave–you may be stuck somewhere for a while.

Insider's tip two. I recently had an appointment with a senior executive at one of the largest search firms in Manhattan. I left my hotel adequately early. It was a lovely day, so I walked. Having had a laptop stolen from a hotel previously, I was paranoid about leaving my laptop in the room, so I lugged it with me. Since I use a backpack my materials and computer were firmly strapped into place. It was warmer than I expected. I was getting overheated by the time I arrived. He invited me into his lovely office, where I removed my coat, only to see that my expensive, perfectly tailored, starched and ironed dress shirt had wrinkles and sweat marks like it had been worn for a weekend in Reppongi by a salary man on an expense account. The moral is to not let your heavy shoulder bag or backpack spoil your appearance.

<u>Dressing for success</u>

Meetings with executive recruiters or employers require conservative business apparel. For men, that generally means a navy or charcoal suit, white or blue regular (not-button-down) collar shirt and lace-up shoes.

The rules for women have loosened up some so that it is fine to look feminine. However, dressier shoes are required. If you chose not to wear a pants suit, the length of your dress or skirt must be appropriate. (Even if you have legs that you think compete with twenty-somethings, you really don't want to show them off in a job interview unless you are applying at Hooters).

There are a few places where these rules are relaxed. First, if you live and work in Silicon Valley, kakis and a blazer may be acceptable – but you should confirm that in advance. Second, in the fashion industry, both men and women may need to dress less conservatively-but more stylishly-to indicate your awareness of current trends. Since the presumption of the hiring employer is that the younger candidate is hipper, make sure that you do your style and fashion review. (But remember, you are the adult and you should look and act like one).

Chapter 5 Advantage

"Now the general who wins a battle makes many calculations in his temple ere the battle is fought…"   SunTzu The Art of War

You are officially warned: a job search is going to be exhausting. If you have had to find work before, you know how challenging, difficult, discouraging and occasionally humiliating it can be. If you haven't looked for work recently, or if you are that rarest and most blest of individuals that has never had to find a new position, you will quickly learn that finding a job is harder than working at a job.

By now you may be anxious to make something happen. You may be facing money problems. You need to find a new job and get back to work. Being out of work may be damaging your self-esteem or self-worth. Your spouse may be unhappy about the situation. But you must complete some further preparation before moving into the execution phase.

The first milestone is to create momentum. You will create momentum by generating thousands of impressions. That will be done by making hundreds, perhaps thousands of phone calls, sending thousands of digital messages and mailing thousands of résumés. Yes, I said thousands. Harnessing the power of your personal computer, smart phone and the Internet and developing an arsenal of special-purpose communication tools will enable the construction of a personal communication network.

By the time your campaign is fully underway you will make 5,000 or more impressions.

You don't know 5,000 people? Don't know how to create 5,000 impressions? Well that's why we are here-to help you generate 5,000–or perhaps many more, impressions, and thereby getting you noticed by hundreds of businesses[2] until you find a new position.

Objective: get interviews with individuals who can hire you.

Don't let that short simple objective just slide by. Soak it in for a minute: the goal of most of the activities you will undertake in your job search is to get in front of a decision maker. Then, your exercise and personal appearance programs will neutralize your age handicap and your superior experience will enable you to out-position your younger, inexperienced opponents.

<u>Tactics</u>

Tactic one: build the contact lists.

Time to gather all the data you possess that can help. You are going to find that you have a much deeper, richer and more robust resources than you thought. At this stage in your life, you probably have:

- · A Rolodex
- · A card file
- · A Christmas card list
- · A phone list
- · Two or more association membership lists
- · A church membership directory
- · Employee phone books
- · LinkedIn Connections
- · An alumni directory
- · One or more email address books in Outlook, Goldmine, Seibel, Lotus Notes, Plaxico, Yahoo Mail, Google Mail (Gmail), Hotmail, Sales Force, LinkedIn or the like
- · Facebook friends

This tactic takes *advantage* of your age–if you are fifty-five you certainly should have met more people than someone who is thirty-five! Your contacts should be more robust, and more successful than someone younger.

Carefully study and then organize your contacts. Take the time to enter them into an electronic address book carefully and completely. Enter all the information you have – home and work addresses, email addresses, work, home and cell phone numbers and so on. Look them up on LinkedIn to fill in the blanks. *If you are missing information, do not call or email your contact yet!* You must have the message you want to deliver fully formed and skillfully crafted first.

Not up to 2,000 yet? Don't worry, we are going to create many more names
and addresses, and utilize technology to multiply your contacts.

Don Reid, a veteran executive recruiter, conducts a career transition
workshop in Franklin TN. Don introduced me to the power of the American
City Business Journals company. This company publishes biweekly business
newspapers for most of the larger cities in the country. Each issue has a list of
the largest *somethings* for each city. That is, the largest architects, the largest
nursing homes, the largest system integrators, etc. Not only do they rank a
different industry each week, the rankings contain revenue, office address
and phone number, the CEO's name and the website address.

Each year those individual weekly lists are published as a book of lists for the
city. Most community libraries will have a copy in the research materials
area. Or, these annual books of lists can be bought directly–see
www.bizjournals.com. When I was looking for a new opportunity, I bought
the books for the cities where I most wanted to work: Dallas, Nashville and
Atlanta. Here are some examples from those books of lists: The Largest:

- Employers

- Advertising agencies

- Retained search firms

- Restaurant chains

- Commercial real estate brokers

- Banks

- Hospitals

- Private companies

- Public companies

While researching for this book, I was reminded how almost every industry
periodical compiles its annual ranking of participants in the industry it

covers. <u>Builder Online</u> (<u>www.builderonline.com</u>) ranks the largest home builders each year. <u>Furniture Today</u> ranks the largest home furniture manufacturers every year. Almost every issue of <u>Business Insurance</u> has a list – the largest:

· Third party claims administrators,

· Insurance brokers

· Employee assistance providers

· Disability insurers

· Reinsurers

· Pension administrators, etc.

These lists will help you to identify at least dozens, if not hundreds, of target employers.

If you plan to change to a new industry, or if you plan to stay in the industry you are in, these rankings give you a shopping list of firms to consider.

LinkedIn (<u>www.linkedin.com</u>) has become the social network for professionals. If you are the rare person who isn't a member, you must join tonight. Or, if you are but haven't taken it that seriously, you need to target creating hundreds (yes, hundreds) of connections. You upload your contacts into the LinkedIn database, and send them invitations to join. Most likely you will find that most of your contacts are already LinkedIn users. Your contacts sign up and add their contacts, and so on. There are millions of registrants throughout the world. You then can message a degree or two away– hat is– you can message a contact of one of your contacts. This will come in very handy when we discuss Directed Networking. LinkedIn is usually the fastest place to get current information on your contacts: most everyone keeps their LinkedIn profiles current.

Now you see how, by combing all your contacts with public lists, we can quickly get to hundreds of names and addresses. Later, we will exploit technology to multiply these contacts to create several thousand impressions. To do that, however, you need to put these into digital format. I'm an Outlook user, and find it just fine for my needs. Many others, in particular skilled sales and marketing executives, prefer Goldmine or Act. Both are powerful contact managers, and I wouldn't quibble. However, the examples I'll use later on how to use Microsoft Word with Outlook might not work if you are using a different tool kit. However, you may already know how to work around any connectivity issues, or find that the power of other tools offsets any linkage disadvantage. Up to you. But you need to put this contact information into some kind of a usable data base.

Tactic two: develop the messages

The single most important message to communicate is your valuable experience. Through basic training, you are offsetting some of the physical manifestations of aging. In this phase of the marketing campaign, you will emphasize the overwhelming value of the accumulated experience, knowledge and wisdom that you have that your younger job competitors simply cannot have developed.

To do this, you MUST create a list of at least 20 accomplishments in your career. These must be explicitly described and as quantitative as possible. Exhibit V-1 shows some examples to help stimulate your thinking and memory. Of course, if you can come up with many more, that is even better, because that makes it easy for you to customize résumés and cover letters with hard–hitting results.

Exhibit 5-1 Sample Accomplishments

Increased revenue in the salty snack category 27% with new advertising, point-of-sale and packaging program.

Developed business plan and raised $10 million from highly-regarded venture capital firms.

Used six sigma black belt skills to reduce manufacturing defects in fractional horsepower product lines by 40% with no increase in unit cost.

Drove 14% sales increase in the Northeast sales district by improving sales call effectiveness and relationship selling.

Participated in the engineering task team that brought six new devices to market in one year, resulting in a 10% market share gain.

Consolidated back-office operations from four locations to one, saving $500,000 per year.

Replaced traditional indemnity insurance program with PPO and cafeteria design, saving $700 per employee per year for a total savings of $350,000.

Wrote new code in Java replacing old legacy code, allowing direct customer access to obtain inventory status and place orders. Online orders were $1.5 million in the first year, reducing cost in customer service by $75,000 and order entry errors by 20%.

Lead SAP implementation team, completed installation of distribution and control modules on time and on budget in 18 locations.

Reevaluated depreciation and expense policy, creating $100,000 in tax savings.

Negotiated new travel contracts, reducing air fare and hotel costs $75,000 in first six months.

Managed all phases of west coast expansion including finding office space, negotiating a lease, hiring initial staff, and purchasing equipment.

Identified a new supplier for polymers, saving $4 million over life of contract.

Managed site selection and construction of new $60 million slurry facility, which was constructed under budget and opened on time.

Created new field sales training program featuring faster feedback to request for quotes, resulting in five percentage point market share gain.

Conducted market research that isolated critical decision factors for deodorant product; resulting advertising campaign improved awareness 33%.

Installed faster machine set-up and changeover process, reducing factory downtime 15%.

Negotiated new labor agreement with reduced post-retirement benefits, saving in excess of $1 million per year.

Trained field maintenance staff on quality techniques and simultaneously rolled-out wireless access to parts inventory, reducing service call time by 25%.

Outsourced payroll and human resources function, saving $300,000 per year.

Prepared the winning RFP's for three potential national accounts, and won sales person of the year award.

Successfully defended the company against class action lawsuit after drop in share price.

Increased the productivity in customer service sufficiently that seven new field offices serving 2,000 new accounts were added with no increase in customer service staff.

Changed advertising placements, saving $50,000 per year while increasing the cumulative impressions.

Consolidated office supply purchasing with an online vendor, saving $60,000.

As a team member in a shop-floor automation project, created vendor selection criteria, evaluated proposals, negotiated vendor and consultant contracts, and implemented system in eighteen months, producing a 20% improvement in on-time deliveries while reducing defects 8%.

Recruited, trained and maintained a Pan-European management sales team that grew market share in every country we entered in a highly competitive technology market.

Was salesperson of the year for southern district, increasing customer base by 19% and sales by 49%.

Improved welding process, reducing defective welds by 19% and customer returns 27%.

Designed new grant applications obtaining new federal grants totaling $750,000.

Opened ten new stores on-time and on-budget.

Installed an applicant tracking system enabling us to reduce time from job posting to hiring by 22%.

Developed new e-commerce and websites using responsive design.

Did these example accomplishments get you going?

Remember, accomplishments must be specific and measurable. Frequently, when I ask a job candidate to describe key accomplishments, he responds with his objectives or responsibilities. As an example, I once interviewed a candidate for a senior sales position. I asked him his key accomplishments in his sales role with his last employer. He replied that he was responsible for sales to all North American technology and telecommunications clients. When I further pursued the question, I received a similarly unsatisfying answer. While other members of our management team were enthusiastic supporters of his candidacy, his inability to distinguish between his duties and his results turned me off. Incidentally, he was over fifty and out of work. Chances are he hadn't practiced interviewing, and certainly hadn't created a list of his twenty most significant accomplishments.

To get started on developing your accomplishments, write four or five for each position you have had. If you have some significant accomplishments not associated with work, include them. (Examples, raised $4 million in alumni campaign to fund Distinguished Chair of Neurology; or was awarded one year full scholarship to study Japanese at the University of Tokyo). Target writing thirty, but absolutely don't stop until you have at least twenty.

Insider tip: craft your key accomplishments right now. Then set them aside for 48 hours, and then review them again at that time. During that review, concentrate on "punching up" the language. If your career is in advertising, public relations or marketing, this shouldn't be a challenge. However, if you come from an accounting or engineering background, this may sound too much like bragging. Remember, the goal of this aspect of your marketing campaign is to get an interview, and to position you as an experienced person who can join the organization and make an immediate impact.

Insider tip two: The bigger the numbers you can support in your accomplishments, the better your chances. (Note the use of large numbers in Exhibit 5-1 previously.)

Insider tip three: use power words to describe your accomplishments: managed, led, directed, created, drove, implemented, installed, supervised, selected, recruited, built, cut, oversaw, and reduced.

Insider tip four: use the active voice at least two-thirds of the time. Remember freshman English? Voice matters. Active voice: "I led the project team that integrated the Northeast acquisition in seven months, generating $8 million in annual savings". Passive voice: "The Northeast acquisition was integrated by a project team which I led".

The step of writing and organizing your accomplishments is exceptionally important in finding a new position. Do you have a friend or a business associate who you know will talk straight to you? Won't pull any punches? Have her review your list. Check that each one is measurable and written concisely but powerfully. You have worked longer than your youthful competitors, so you should have accomplished more and have more to talk about!

Once you have developed your accomplishments, type them up in at least 14 point type. Print this list and keep it handy because we will refer to it frequently in this program until you find your next position and start work. And you will find yourself referring back to it even more frequently.

<u>Practice using your accomplishments</u>

Practice answering two typical interview questions:

1. Looking back over your career, what are the two or three accomplishments you are most proud of?

2. Name an important contribution you made in each of your last three positions.

Practice these questions until you can recite the answers smoothly, easily, seemingly naturally, but concisely.

Tactic three: develop your critical scripts

During WWII, Winston Churchill and Franklin D Roosevelt rallied the troops abroad and the supporters at home with carefully crafted and skillfully delivered speeches. Those speeches still inspire us today, more than half a century later.

While your speeches aren't likely to be heard and read by millions, you must craft them with the care that presidential speech writers use. For many, if not most of the contacts you will make, you will have an extremely short time to make an impression, and therefore the message you deliver must be skillfully crafted and perfectly delivered.

You will need three scripts:

1. A touch base script
2. A cold call script
3. A network referral script

Additionally, you will need a practiced answer to "why did you leave your last job?

In the remainder of this chapter you will develop your touch-base script. (You will develop your networking script as part of the exercises in Chapter 14 and your cold-calling script in Chapter 16). There are multiple objectives for the touch base script. One is simply help update your contact records. Americans are mobile; many of the addresses, email addresses and phone numbers you have are out of date. Obviously a clean list to work from is required. Second, touch-base calling is great practice before moving to the more challenging world of network calling and cold calling. And finally, it will take repeated impressions to incite action. This will create the first impression, and begin the building of your giant network (more on that later).

As I started my search, my touch base script was:

High this is.....(last name if they didn't know me well, or we haven'ttalked in a while). I'm just calling to touch base. I've left Company X, and I'm beginning to look for a new CFO position. I just wanted to get all my contact information up to date. Is your address still ___________ and your email _________? By the way, I'm trying to find Mark and Richard from our old days together. Do you know how to reach them?

<u>Touch base phone calls and emails</u>

In this phase, you are going to make the initial contact by phone or email, letting people know that you looking for a new career opportunity. However, at this point you are not asking them to take any action other than being alert for something that might be appropriate for you, but the real purpose of the contact is to get your contact list current (and to begin the repetitive impressions that will cumulatively result in your finding a new position).

However, before you begin making these calls, two additional items must be in order. First is a good working draft of your résumé and, second is prepared answers to certain difficult questions. In the next chapter, we will work on your résumé.

As you make your touch base calls, two things will happen frequently – you'll be asked what happened in your last position, and you'll be asked for your résumé. Your answer and the quality of your preparation will be critical to the impression you make. You must script your answer and rehearse it until you can say it naturally. And you can't begin making the calls until you have your résumé in good order. I know this delay is very frustrating for action-oriented individuals. However, poorly prepared documents or weak answers at this stage will damage your search and lengthen the amount of time required to find a new position. At this stage in your life, you should have learned a little patience and self-control. This is a good time to use it.

As an example, you'll need an answer to the "what happened" question. You need to prepare it and practice it. Here are a couple of samples:

"As you know, ABC Corporation had a significant downsizing, affecting 2,000 people. These things happen nowadays. I had a great four years there, and I really enjoyed it, but it's time to find a new career home".

"I had a great ride for 10 years at ABC, but there was a change at the CEO level, and he wanted to pick his own marketing guy. They treated me fairly, and now it is time for me to find a new position".

Your answer must:

- Be factually accurate (after all, the best companies-the kind you want to work for- will certainly check out your story)
- Be delivered calmly and unemotionally. (After all, you lost a *job*, not

your dog. That is why they call it *work*.)

· Forestall other questions. You don't want to invite lots of follow-up questions on this topic: it is not why you called. You are interested in the future. Make your answer complete and fulfilling, so that your questioner doesn't feel compelled to follow-up, or feel that he just got handled by you rather than receiving a satisfactory answer to an important question.

Spend a few minutes now developing your touch base script. Remember, it is simple and straightforward. You are simply updating your contact details – phone numbers, email addresses, mailing addresses. If you've lost touch with someone–a former coworker, an old boss, or a recruiter, ask others who may know them how they can be reached as you make your phone calls. When done repeatedly, it will build your network.

Remember, you are still not ready to make those touch base calls just yet – we need to get your résumé in good shape first. About a seventy-five word script is the maximum, and fifty to sixty is fine – so don't get wordy or too talkative–you want to hear from them. Let them talk. Engage them in a conversation–which means listening *at least* half the time.

Got your touch base drafted? Then practice saying it out loud, as if you are making the actual call. Listen for your tone– his *must* be delivered with energy–you are excited about a new opportunity. Stand up while practicing delivering your script-that almost always creates more projection and enthusiasm.

Now, do the same thing for the "what happened" speech. Again, seventy-five words are an *absolute* maximum, and you must practice your delivery aloud. You must be convincing– ven your best friend won't pass along a job lead if he senses you are in mourning over the loss of your last position or not emotionally ready to tackle a new assignment.

We are almost ready to start making those contacts, but not quite. In the next chapter we'll polish your résumé to a fine shine and then you'll be ready to launch.

Chapter 6 Marketing

There are voluminous books, consulting services, frequent seminars, professional services and writers dedicated to the topic of résumés. Entire articles (and arguments) parsing the virtues and sins of one, two, three page and longer résumés. And with good reason: for many, if not most, of the prospective employers that you are or become interested in, your résumé and cover letter are the key to obtaining an interview.

<u>Your key marketing document</u>

The résumé is your key advertising and marketing document. In designing an advertising piece, the more one knows about the desired audience, the better the marketing appeal that can be made–and the smarter the media selection can be.   You are going to post résumés to job web sites, hand them out in networking groups, and give them to networking contacts. Each of these audiences has different needs, which you must recognize in designing your c.v. Further, when your research and espionage has identified a real known opportunity, you are going to customize a response *just for that position*.

Given the importance then, of a great résumé, there is no excuse for not having a terrific document. Fortunately, there are tools and techniques to make this a relatively simple process. These tools apply computer power to motorize the process of creating multiple résumés that meet these disparate needs. And these tools make it easy to build on the work you have already done (in Chapter 5), so that creating multiple formats is not much more difficult than creating one. And, you avoid wasting lots of time listening to people tell you that your résumés is too long or too short, because you are going to have a variety of lengths.

Objective: The objective of a résumé is to get an interview. It is that simple. *Do not let anything else you read or anyone confuse this objective.*

Tactic: Create an assortment of résumés.

Here is a description of the résumés you are going to create:

1. The one-pager. The one-pager is most useful as a leave-behind in a network meeting–a one-on-one session. We will start with the one-pager, and

then leverage that work to create the additional versions you will need. You will find an example one-pager as Exhibit 6-1.

2. The networker. Think of this like the short tax form 1040 EZ. Brief, summarized, insert the key numbers, pay the tax, move on. The short form résumé is also always exactly one page. It is used exclusively in networking *groups* (see Chapter 14) and note networking *groups*–not *networking*.

Exhibit 6-3 presents an example networker. Since the goal is to get an interview, the focus of this document is to describe the kind of position and list target companies that you are interested in. In the meetings of a networking group, you will have the opportunity to share position goals and contacts with others. The more they understand what kind of position, in which industry, etc. that you are seeking, the more they can help.

 3. The e-document.   Job sites are a vital resource to the typical job-seeker, and an essential resource to the information industry job-seeker. Unfortunately, most job sites have unique, extremely time consuming, and limiting methods of data-entry. So, you need to develop a résumé with no special characters, no unusual fonts or visual and highlighting techniques, thereby reducing the time required for job-posting to a minimum. We will strip your résumé of those to create the fastest possible web-site posting form.

4. The industry standard. Exhibit 6-2 presents the industry standard. Two pages, chronological, focused on the accomplishments you built in Chapter 5. Clean, easy to read, no tiny fonts, with crystal clear information on how to reach you by phone, letter or email 24/7.

You will use the industry standard in a variety of settings. It is perfect for a meeting with a search firm executive, for example, because many of them have unnatural hang-ups about résumés longer than two pages. While my view is that this two-page form frequently is inferior to longer ones, my view here isn't relevant–remember our objective–and you aren't trying to get an interview with me! (And we know that inferior products frequently win in the marketplace–many readers of this book are old enough to remember Beta vs. VHS. The technical folks told me that Beta was better–but it didn't win in the marketplace.) The two-page format is so expected that it is a bad idea not to have one and use it. And, once you have the one-pager, the two-pager can be quickly generated anyway.

5. The direct mail piece. If your experience and education justifies it–and if you are over fifty and have steadily advanced in your career it probably does– then create a three–or for exceptional careers–even four- page résumés. Exhibit 6-4 illustrates a longer format.

This format is best employed when you are sending a letter to a hiring executive. I also like to bring this along with me if I'm a candidate and I am going to be interviewed by several executives. You never know what kind of materials they have received or the legibility. Having an easy-to-read, nicely formatted and crisply printed three page document to pass across a desk eliminates all kinds of risks about faxes, or copies of faxes might have. And it contain all of the formatting benefits that today's software provides in the form of bolding, underlining, bullets and numbering.

If a two page format is the gold standard, then you might correctly inquire as to why go to the trouble to create an even longer document. Query: When does this make sense? Answer: When two "if" conditions are met – first, if you are mailing to a company (preferably a person you have identified within the company) – and second, if the sum of your accomplishments, variety of relevant experience and technical skills merit it.

Here are some examples to help you decide if you should have a longer document:

· 	If you have progressed steadily through your career, worked at five or six well known and highly regarded companies, with increasing scope and rising job titles, then by all means you should to highlight those accomplishments. Even more so if the jobs and changes provided unique experience. A friend of mine worked for a large international, well-known consumer packaged goods firm in Asia, then in a higher position with a second CPG firm in South America, and followed that with an even more senior position with another CPG business in the U.S. Informing a reader of this extent of hands-on international expertise combined with increased job responsibility is critical for his résumé to stand out from the mounds of résumés companies receive every day.

·   If you are in the field of information technology, longer résumés have become accepted, because they allow the communication of technical skills, such as the variety of programming languages or data base tools that you have mastered, as well as a listing of key project assignments undertaken as opposed to listing positions, tenure and scope. This informs the reader of the systems you've built and the industries covered. This is particularly appropriate for individuals with extensive experience in consulting firms.

·   For research scientists and the like, indicating the nature, facility, timing and technology employed or developed for projects you participated in or managed is an appropriate method for communicating the strength of your background.

There is another special case résumé that is covered in Chapter 10 on Propaganda, but for now, it is critical to create-at a minimum–both a one and a two page résumé.

At this point you may be thinking that one, or perhaps two at the most, of these documents make sense, and there can't be any good reason to have five different documents. My experience at finding jobs says you are wrong–but more importantly–it doesn't matter what either of us think, because Microsoft, Google and Apple have made it so easy for you to create multiple formats that there is no reason not to!

Using the tools and building blocks in your software and the computer horsepower available to virtually everyone in America, you will get this done far faster than you can imagine. I am surprised at the number of people who don't know that built into Microsoft Word are a variety of templates, including templates for résumés. You find them in the Backstory under the File tab. Open Microsoft Word, click File, then New, then the templates appear. There are two sets: "New résumé samples" and." Résumés and CV's" (Importantly, I used this method to create Exhibit 6-1 from start to finish in under an hour).

In my version of Microsoft Word there are a striking number of other résumé templates and a related wizard. If you are preparing these documents on your own computer, and you registered the Microsoft license agreement in your name, you might also try the "wizard" feature, which is also found in the General Templates.

Insider Tip: Not excited by the template formats that came with your version of Microsoft Word? Go to http://office.microsoft.com/templates. There you will find, as of this writing, fourteen additional general résumé templates, and an astonishing ninety-four position specific templates that you can download and use immediately.

<u>The One-Pager</u>

First, you are going to prepare a One-Page résumé. While I obviously believe that longer résumés are generally better at presenting the career accomplishments of the mature worker, there are some important reasons to create the one-page version. The single most important is that it requires you to be painfully concise. And this skill is critical as you use Twitter (yes, that's coming shortly) to generate publicity and buzz.

Ask any professional writer– particularly advertising or marketing communications writers–and they will tell you that anyone can write long copy. It is more difficult to boil text down to the essentials that can be communicated in seconds. We are in the Facebook, Snapchat and Twitter era. The target audience for your message is bombarded by communications and media-from pop-up ads on the Internet to location-aware smartphone texts to the billboards on their daily commute. You must write in simple declarative sentences that get to the point. This isn't just an electronic media trend; business periodicals too like *Fast Company* and *Inc.* shun the longer articles that previously defined business publications in favor of quick reads.

Spend a few minutes watching cable or network news. Pay particular attention to politicians being interviewed. They know that no matter how much tape is shot during an interview, only a few seconds will make it to the network news. Accordingly, they speak in sound bites–brief, well thought out, even clever. (You didn't think those lines were truly off the cuff did you?) By distilling your c.v.to a single page, you are forced to think in sound bites. This has the ancillary benefit of preparing you for interview questions (we'll cover that in detail later) since your concise statements here will frequently be good answers for questions. And the process of writing and editing may help you remember the key points.

 Exhibit 6-1 presents the one-page format. (Note that résumés have been reformatted for e-readers.)

)05 Central Ave., Nashville TN 37001

615 123 -1234 ·scott@scottkreger.com

;cott Kreger

)bjective

)in a growing consumer goods company where my extensive
:perience at the executive level in brand-building and sales
:neration can make an immediate contribution to revenue and
irnings.

xperience

)04-2015 BigDiamonds.com

ashville TN

VP Marketing

- Increased sales from $14 million to $20 million.

- Created and monitored "look and feel" of website for
consistent message and impact.

- Developed sales associate recruiting and training
programs.

)99-2004 MicroPower San Jose CA & Seoul
VP Sales

> Increased sales to the Global 1,000 by 20% through
> programs targeting CIO's with relationship selling

- Restructured commission system to reward sales growth
and penetration of server market. Results: 30% growth

of server sales with only 5% increase in total commissions.

)94-1999 Progressive Consumer Products

etroit MI

P Sales and Marketing

- Based on detailed market research, designed and introduced a men's fragrance and skin care line.

- Placed that line in three of the four largest upscale department store chains, resulting in significant market share gain.

- Managed a staff of 400 in over 25 countries.

)83-1994 American Boutique

hicago IL

P Advertising and Marketing

- Directed greater spending toward in-store activities, cutting ad spending $2 million while reversing a 2% negative sales trend.

- Started as Advertising Manager; advanced through several positions to the senior marketing position

ducation

)73-1977 University of Memphis
BA – Business Administration
)81-1983 Northwestern University

IBA – Marketing Concentration

In an hour we have developed our first of four documents. (I timed myself–
and I'm certainly not the fastest user of Microsoft Word– and I created this in
exactly 30 minutes.) Let's examine this document closely.

<u>Technical points</u>

As mentioned, this was prepared using the "Chronological résumé traditional
design" template. There are other formats with Word and many more on the
net. It is clean, easy to read, plenty of white space and overall does a good
job.

*Insider tip: many companies are now using an "applicant tracking system"
or ATS. This is particularly true for very fast growing businesses that need to
hire a number of people, or very large headcount companies that need to hire
thousands just to replace turnover (Target or Wal-Mart for example) or
companies concerned about anti-discrimination regulation that need
structured record-keeping. An ATS is typically fed by scanning résumés, not
by key-entering. ATS look for records in a certain order, and can be confused
by complicated font, multiple columns, etc. In particular, those systems look
for name, address and contact information to be in that specific order at the
top of the first page. This format is ideal for an ATS.*

<u>Position objective</u>

The objective is crisp and clear–including clarity as to the position sought.
Scott has a rich background in sales, advertising and marketing. His
preference is for a position in the consumer marketing area as opposed to a
business-to-business marketing position in a company that produces
industrial equipment for industrial users. (Wait a minute– Scott could have
another résumé, couldn't he? And it could target business-to-business
companies). But the reader doesn't know that Scott is using computer power
to target an audience of one–so he thinks Scott's interests align perfectly with
the position he needs to fill).

*Insider tip 2: Whenever you know some job specifics, change your career
objective commensurately so that the reader is instantly aware that his
position is just what you are looking for. (Of course, I absolutely do not want
you to lie, or even exaggerate in this regard – you'll simply end up in a job*

you hate, or even worse, one you aren't qualified for, and end up reading this book again 18 months from now).

<u>Accomplishments</u>

Scott used his accomplishments to illustrate his capabilities. The more he knows about the specifics of the position, the more he can go back to his accomplishments list and pull out the ones most relevant to

<u>Concise</u>

It is tight: all on one page with easy to read font and reasonable margins. This makes a nice marketing piece to leave behind, or an easy mailer when combined with a thoughtful cover letter.

<u>Drawbacks</u>

There are legitimate criticisms of this format. Except for the names of the largest corporations in the world, it is very possible that the reader won't know what some of the companies on the résumé are or what they do. It is very useful then to describe prior employers, and there simply isn't space for that here. Similarly, as shown in an upcoming résumé, we want to have an "Interests" section, and that too is sacrificed for brevity.

<u>Multiple versions</u>

Why would you want or need multiple versions of your résumé? Simple. First, you want to maximize your opportunities by broadening the positions you might be considered for. While you may be the best prepared by education, training, background and experience for a VP of Marketing position, why not take a shot at a Chief Operating role or a Division President position? After all, haven't you reported to a general manager and thought to yourself "I know I could do a better job than he is?" Conversely, if you are a general manager, consider returning to the technical roots of your core experience. Give yourself as many options as possible. Unfortunately, interviewers typecast the person based upon the résumé; as a result you need multiple résumés for multiple opportunities.

Second, since you've been around a while, you have far more accomplishments than a more junior person (as you documented in Chapter 5). As you learn about a particular position, you *must* change your accomplishments on your résumé to highlight directly relevant results.

Third, you want to take the customer's viewpoint whenever possible to improve your target marketing. If you know that the person you want to reach has a short attention span, then you should respond with a one-page C.V. On the other hand, if you are contacting a hiring manager that your espionage (covered in Chapter 19) has told you is a very analytical, thoughtful person, then, by all means, use more pages to create a powerful direct marketing piece.

<u>The Industry Standard</u>

Now we are going to create The Industry Standard Résumé. And we'll do it in record time by taking our one-pager and simply expanding it. My recommendation for this conversion is to add an "accomplishment" section to the top to highlight critical successes, and then add some job description detail to each position. That is the important data we omitted to squeeze into the one-page format.

With the editorial freedom of two pages, we'll give the reader some clarity on what the specifics of each job were. And, I've added an accomplishment or two to each key position. Note that the additions focused on the most recent jobs, not those in the distant past. Scott's job history includes only five employers – uncommonly stable. You may have ten or more. (I do). If three or four of those were short stints of a technical job nature, you may want to combine them at the end. For example, if you were in insurance sales out of college, and you had sales rep positions with three different insurers, you may simply want to combine them. A summary such as: 1965-1970 a sales representative for Northwestern Life, New York Life and Allstate, should be fine. You don't want to omit employers or years of service (at least, not on the Industry Standard). If someone is really interested in the details of your work experience thirty- five years ago, let them ask.

It is essential, however, to hold the Industry Standard to two pages – and don't yield to the temptation to use a smaller font. The premium we placed on brevity isn't suspended here. The end product must still be very clean.

2005 Central Ave., Nashville TN 37001 · (615) 123 -1234· scott@scottkreger.com

Scott Kreger

Objective

Join a growing consumer goods company where my extensive experience at the executive level in brand-building and sales generation can make an immediate contribution to revenue and earnings.

Accomplishments

- For major, multinational PC OEM, maintained constant dollar marketing and advertising budget (declining from 2% of sales to .5%) while revenue grew an average of 30% per year.

- Assumed responsibility for $30 mil advertising and promotion budget for high-end ladies' apparel chain. Conducted search for new agency, redirected larger part of budget to in-store promotion, changed media mix. Reversed 2% negative same store sales trend to 4% positive trend, while cutting spending by $2 mil.

- For multinational consumer products company, conducted detailed market research for opportunities for men's fragrance and skin care products. Drove product development process to create new designer lines aimed at young men with growing incomes. Product was introduced in three of the US' four upscale department stores with all displaying full assortments. In this highly volatile market, this product is still holding market share.

Experience

2004-2015 BigDiamonds.com

Nashville TN

BigDiamonds is a privately held $20 million online jewelry firm.

EVP Marketing

Responsible for all marketing, advertising and promotion and customer service activities.

- Increased sales from $14 million to $20 million.

§ Created and monitored "look and feel" of website for consistent message and impact.

§ Developed sales associate recruiting and training programs.

§ Prepared and delivered presentations to the venture capital community that raised a third funding round of $20 million to sustain growth.

1999-2004 MicroPower

San Jose CA & Seoul Korea

A $15 billion PC OEM. Public: Korean Exchange.
EVP Sales

Global sales responsibility for all channels. Managed a sales force of over 300 located in twenty countries in fifty sales offices.

- Increased sales to the Global 1,000 by 20% through programs targeting CIO's with relationship selling supported by fast RFP responses.

- Restructured commission system to reward sales growth and penetration of server market. Results: 30% growth of server sales with only 5% increase in total commissions.

1994-1999 Progressive Consumer Products

Detroit MI

A $2.4 billion consumer products firm. Public: NYSE
VP Sales and Marketing

Responsible for all sales and marketing functions in the personal care group. Professional staff of over 100; direct sales and sales support over 300, total budget responsibility in excess of $100 million.

- Based on detailed market research, designed and introduced a mens' fragrance and skin care line.

  § Placed that line in three of the four largest upscale department store chains, resulting in significant market share gain.

  § Managed a staff of 400 in over 25 countries.

- Grew market share in seven of the nine major categories of the personal care group.

1983-1994 American Boutique

Chicago IL

A $700 million revenue, designer-oriented ready-to-wear chain.
VP Advertising and Marketing

- Directed greater spending toward in-store activities, cutting ad spending $2 million while reversing a 2% negative sales trend.

- Started as Advertising Manager; advanced through several positions to the senior marketing position.

1977-1981 Swift

A $3 billion food and consumer products company
Sales Trainee/Sales Representative
- Developed area marketing plans

- Won "Rookie of the Year" award

Education

1973-1977 University of Memphis
BBA– Business Administration

1981-1983   Northwestern University
MBA– Marketing Concentration

Other interests

Mountain biking, ocean kayaking and reading

Other interests

Note that I've added a section on Scott's other interests. Scott actually has a longer list of hobbies and interests. But if that include stamp collecting and playing with his grandkids, he is wise to indicate his vigor and stamina by selecting those active ones rather than the tamer, intellectual pursuits. Part of winning against younger candidates is using our wisdom isn't it?

The Networker

The Networker is a highly specialized document. As your search for a new position goes along, you will likely attend or join some networking groups, and you will certainly meet with individuals in classic networking one-on-one meetings. On those occasions, you may want a different marketing piece: one that stimulates others to think of positions that might be appropriate for you. Or that triggers ideas of contacts from their network that you should meet.

As shown on Exhibit 6-3, this is a no-nonsense, one-page summary of the kind of position that you are qualified for and what employers you want to contact.

Exhibit 6-3-Networking Group Résumé

Scott Kreger

2005 Central Ave

Nashville TN 37001

Phone (123) 123-1234; Cell (123) 123-1234;

 email scott@scottkreger.com

Objective: Join a growing consumer goods company where my extensive experience at the executive level in brand-building and sales generation can make an immediate contribution to revenue and earnings.

Target Companies:

· Uniliver	· Proctor & Gamble	· Kao
· M&M Mars	· Levi's	· Black & Decker
· AutoZone		

Target Locations:

· San Francisco	· Atlanta	· Boston
· Northern VA	· London	· Tokyo

Skills: Managing advertising for effectiveness, finding new market opportunities,

cost-conscious marketing management. Deep, in-country international experience.

Accomplishments:

- For a major multinational PC OEM, maintained constant dollar marketing and advertising budget (declining from 2% of sales to .5%) while revenue grew an average of 30% per year.

- Assumed responsibility for $30 mil advertising and promotion budget for high-end ladies' apparel chain. Conducted search for new agency, redirected larger part of budget to in-store promotion, changed media mix. Reversed 2% negative same store sales trend to 4% positive trend, while cutting spending by $2 mil.

- For a multinational consumer products company, conducted detailed market research for opportunities for men's' fragrance and skin care products. Drove product development process to create new designer lines aimed at young men with growing incomes. Product was introduced in three of the US' four largest upscale department stores with all customers displaying full assortments. In this highly volatile market, this product is still holding market share.

EVP – Marketing at Big Diamonds – successful Internet retail site marketing high-end gemstones to consumers.

<u>Education</u>
BA Marketing – University of Memphis 1977
MBA- Northwestern – 1983

<u>Other interests</u>
Mountain biking, ocean kayaking and reading

As the Exhibit shows, this is very different from our other documents. There is no job history prior to the last one. No fluff stuff. This straight-to-the-point document enables your networking meeting peers to quickly remember any opportunities that they are aware of that might be on-target for you, and to evaluate future opportunities they learn of.

Since this isn't likely to be scanned or entered into an automated system, it is possible to change the format to use different styling as needed.

<u>The e-document</u>

Some of the formatted résumés in Microsoft Word note that they are designed to be uploaded. This is a nice advantage. While, in my view, one frequently sacrifices fast and effective communication with these formats, the risk of getting lost in a data warehouse with no means of being found is far worse.

Save more complicated styles for individual, face-to-face meetings.

<u>Use of keywords</u>

If you haven't had to look for work for a while, one of the key differences from just five or six years ago is the increased importance of keywords in an on-line search. Employers and recruiters may use keywords to sort through the millions of résumés posted online, or the thousands of responses they get to an online job posting. Let's use an illustration. Employer A is about to launch on the implementation of an Oracle application suite and database. Employer A goes to the Monster.com site and searches for candidates whose résumé includes "Oracle", "database", "project management" and "application development". Viola! Employer A has a list of job-seekers who have a least some of the qualifications it is looking for.

Your e-document must contain those keywords that are most relevant to the position you want next. If you consider yourself an expert in compliance with Dodd Frank regulations, for example, or project management, both currently in-demand skills, then your résumés should show that in some way.

Increasingly, I'm seeing job seekers simply listing buzzwords at the bottom of their online résumés. It looks a little unsightly – perhaps even ungainly, but I'll admit that it is effective, and I wasn't put off by it so much that I wouldn't consider the candidate. You should consider preparing a list that has the best buzzwords from your background and industry.

Things like:

Six sigma black belt
Sarbanes-Oxley
SAP
Project management
Multilingual
JD Edwards
Oracle
PowerPoint
CPA
MBA
MD
JD
Homeland security
Firewall
Security
Shared services
Government sales
Large account
National accounts
Java
Perl
Scripting
Internal audit
Security clearance
Private equity
Venture capital
Social
E-commerce
Dynamics
Salesforce.com

CRM
PHP
HTML
WordPress
Mobile applications
Dodd Frank
Omni-channel

Those are examples of terms that reflect currently in-demand positions. Spend a few minutes to develop the list of hot topic terms and concepts in your field. If they aren't already included in your text, sprinkle a few in at the end. You don't want to miss a great opportunity because the bot trolling the web missed your outstanding capabilities because you simply didn't show up on its filtered results.

Insider tip: you can add key words like those to the bottom of your résumé and then hide them by highlighting them, clicking on the font button and changing the font to white.

<u>The Direct Mail Piece</u>

We take liberties with the direct mail piece. [3] Specifically, we let the document extend to three, or for the rare, remarkable career, four pages. (Let's pause here for a minute to define *remarkable*. That would include positions as CEO of public companies, or Members of Congress, or partners in major law, private equity, CPA or venture capital firms, etc. If that isn't you, hold to two pages.) Start construction of your direct mail piece with your Industry Standard résumé. Carefully identify those accomplishments that can be emphasized with action statements and color commentary. Or, think about the words you edited out to get down to two pages. Were there sentences that you felt were more effective with longer copy? Add them back.

But, don't do this just to be wordy or satisfy your desire to follow this book too literally. If you are completely satisfied that your résumé is already very effective, and another page won't be that helpful, by all means don't spend time here.

Exhibit 6-4-The Direct Mail Piece

2005 Central Avenue, Nashville TN 37001   Cell:(123) 123-1234; email:scott@scottkreger.com

Scott Kreger

<u>Objective</u>

Join a growing consumer goods company where my extensive experience at the executive level in brand-building and sales generation can make an immediate contribution to revenue and earnings.

<u>Accomplishments</u>

- Conducted market research for a line of fragrances and skin care for men, then managed the product development process to create a line for young men with rising incomes. Introduced the products into three of the four leading better department stores. Annual sales now in excess of $100 million and the products continue to gain share in a very competitive segment.

- Maintained a constant dollar marketing and advertising budget (declining from 2% of sales to .5) while revenue grew an average of 30% per year.

- Assumed responsibility for $30 mil advertising and promotion budget for high-end ladies' apparel chain. Conducted search for new agency, redirected larger part of budget to in-store promotion, changed media mix. Reversed 2% negative same store sales trend to 4% positive trend, while cutting spending by $2 million.

<u>Experience</u>

2004-2015 BigDiamonds.com Nashville, TN
A $20 million online jewelry firm. Privately held.

EVP Marketing
Responsible for all marketing, advertising and promotion and customer service activities.
- Increased sales from $14 million to $20 million.
- Created and monitored "look and feel" of website for consistent message and impact.
- Developed sales associate recruiting and training programs.
- Created mobile version of website
- Prepared and delivered presentations to the venture capital community that raised a third funding round of $20 million to sustain growth.

1999-2004 MicroPower San Jose, CA & Seoul, Korea
A $15 billion PC OEM   Public: Korean Exchange

EVP Sales

Global sales responsibility for all channels. Managed a sales force of over 300 located in twenty countries in fifty sales offices.

- Increased Fortune Global 1,000 direct sales by 20% through programs targeting CIO's with relationship selling supported by fast RFP responses.

- Restructured commission system to reward sales growth and penetration of server market. Results: 30% growth of server sales with only 5% increase in total commissions.

1994-1999 Progressive Consumer Products Detroit, MI
A $2.4 billion consumer products firm. Public: NYSE
VP Sales and Marketing
Responsible for all sales and marketing functions in the personal care group. Professional staff of over 100; direct sales and sales support over 300, total budget responsibility in excess of $100 million.

- Based on detailed market research, designed and introduced a new men's fragrance and skin care line.
- Placed that line in three of the four largest upscale department store chains, resulting in significant market share gain.
- Managed a staff of 400 in over 25 countries.
- Grew market share in seven of the nine major categories of the personal care group.

1983-1994 American Boutique Chicago, IL
A $700 million revenue, designer-oriented ready-to-wear chain.

VP – Advertising and Marketing
Responsible for market positioning, market research and all advertising and sales promotion activity.

- Conducted search for new advertising agency, improving advertising reach while reducing costs.
- Directed greater spending to in-store activities, cutting ad spending $2million while reversing 2% negative sales trend.
- Started as Advertising Manager; advanced through several positions to the senior marketing position.

1977-1981 Swift Chicago, IL

A $3 billion food and consumer products company.

Sales Trainee/Sales Representative
- Developed area marketing plans.
- § Won "Rookie of the Year" award.

Education

1977 University of Memphis Memphis, TN
- B.A. Business Administration

1983
- MBA Northwestern University Chicago, IL

Interests

Mountain biking, ocean kayaking and reading.

Personal

Married; two grown children. Would consider relocation both in the U.S. and internationally.

<u>Formatting</u>

Just a follow-up on formatting. I love Amazon. I love e-books. And I love Amazon Kindle. As I state elsewhere in this book, I'm a committed reader. I've been a long-time Amazon customer and buy hard-back books regularly. I'm a Barnes & Noble shopper and buy books from them frequently. I also have a Kindle and buy a lot of eBooks from Amazon. But e-books are limited in capability to reproduce fonts, bolding and tables. The preceding résumés have been stripped of those features. I actually like those features and believe, if used properly, help communicate selected elements to the reader. The absence of that reflects my need to format for e-book publication, not my opposition to them. That is not a blanket endorsement of Wing-Ding fonts and crazy font sizes. You are the experienced, practical, level-headed job applicant, remember?

<u>Career facts</u>

By now, you are sick of lists, but you've got another to prepare.

In addition to your résumé, the other tool you will need at your disposal is your facts list. Your facts list contains those key data points that someone might ask for and you want to demonstrate command of the facts.

Examples of questions that need a factual answer:

How many people were in the total organization that you managed?
What was your budget?
How much capital expenditure did you authorize?
What were the sales and profits of the division you managed?
What was the cycle time for your manufacturing operation?
How many stores were in your chain?
What was the square footage of those warehouses?
How many different items did your business produce?
How many countries were you operating in?
What was the largest budget you ever managed?
How big was the accounts receivable portfolio you were responsible for?
How many SKUs were in the warehouse?
How big was your advertising budget? How was it spent by media type?

How long did the system implementation take?
How many salesmen were in each territory?
How big was the truck fleet?
How long did it take to change that process?
What was your compensation in that position?
What was your grade point average?
Just how many new products were introduced per year?
How many programmers and analysts were assigned to that project?
What is the largest organization you've ever managed?
How many policies were in force?
What was the turnover rate in that organization?
What was your supervisor's name in that position?
What were the names of the people who reported to you in that position?
How many people did you train?
How many people did you recruit?
How big was the 401(k) plan in dollars and participants?
How many health care claims were processed per day?
How many patients were treated each day?
How long did it take from design through completion of construction?
How was your commission plan structured?
How long did it take to close the books and report results?
How many units were produced each day?
Describe the process for software testing before it was put into production.
What was the defect rate?
How many nodes were on the network?
How big was the server farm?
How many lines of code were in those programs?
How did you know that you were PCI compliant?
What was the inventory turnover?
How many years were you there?
What was your web traffic?
What was the sales closing rate?
How long did construction take?
What was the combined loss ratio?
What was the credit approval rate?
What was the customer churn rate?
What was the customer penetration rate?

How did the margin by product vary?
Who was on the Board?
What was the portfolio turnover?
What were the assets under management?
What was the bad-debt charge-off rate?
What were the loans outstanding?
How many RFP's were answered annually?
What was the effective tax rate?
How long did it take to develop the Android version?
How did you decide which applications went to the cloud and which were hosted on your servers?
Were you responsible for both new sales prospecting and account maintenance?

I'm sure by now you get the idea – there is certain information that your interviewer will request to determine how small or large the area you were in was, how good your grasp of data is and to validate that you really did what you claim. For each position you show on your résumé, you need to compile the relevant facts, memorize as much as possible and keep the rest handy.

Once you have completed your résumé, have a polished touch-base script and have practiced answers to the "what happened in your last position" question, then you can begin touch-base calls. But, are you completely clear on the type of position that you want, what firms you would like to work for where you want to live? If not, you might want to spend some time on Chapter 10 before beginning your contact campaign. Otherwise you are ready to move from marketing campaign planning to campaign implementation. The balance of this book addresses identifying and reaching target employers, managing your financial condition effectively and preparing for interviews.

If you've followed the plan this far, you now have a base established and you are ready to go find that next great position.

Chapter 7 Multi-channel

"After we have thought out everything carefully in advance and have sought and found without prejudice the most plausible plan, we must not be ready to abandon it at the slightest provocation. Should this certainty be lacking, we must tell ourselves that nothing is accomplished in warfare without daring...
" Karl von Clausiwitz

We've learned that the new world of business requires multi-channel operation. To compete effectively, retailers can no longer just offer their merchandise in stores, but also need to offer it on the Internet via e-commerce, and on mobile devices. Manufacturers and service companies now need to monitor Twitter and Yelp for customer complaints, have a social media strategy, and maintain an effective website.

Similarly, you will now manage a multi-channel communication programs. Time management becomes critical as your campaign for a new position moves into full swing. Just as you had to balance tradeoffs between work and family, personal development and personal service while you were working, you will have to set priorities for your daily and weekly activities and make those same tradeoffs as you look for work.

In Chapter 3 – The Abstract you saw an overview of this program to help you find a new position expeditiously. Using this chapter as a guide, you will build your detailed plan to obtain your next position. Further, in this chapter, we develop two timelines:

· A one hundred day plan to launch and control your overall campaign, and
· A weekly plan to help focus on the critical tasks of finding a new position.

I am told that Rudy Popovich, the highly successful coach of the San Antonio Spurs, has a sign in his office that reads: "Don't be in a hurry to win". If there is a key mistake commonly made by the new job-seeker, it is rushing into the job market before being fully prepared and ready. We've spent considerable time now readying you for these next steps. If you are currently out of work, use this chapter to review the actions you are currently taking–use this information as a checklist to make sure that you are not only covering all the basics, but also to check that your techniques are fully developed and military grade.

If you are currently employed, but see the writing on the wall because:

- · Of ongoing financial deterioration by your employer or industry,
- · Of downsizing happening currently in your firm, or
- · Because your boss is a jerk,

then this chapter is of critical value, since you can begin many of these activities while still employed. Three times in my career I've used situations just like that to find new positions.

Once, after a hostile takeover, it was apparent to me that it was only a matter of time until I would be let go. I began my marketing campaign, and, when indeed I was let go, I started a new position 48 hours later! Later in my career, as my relationship with an immature CEO worsened, I quietly began searching for a new position. It took about five months of very long hours balancing work and job search, but I found an equivalent position, and avoided getting fired, which was otherwise inevitable. And finally, finding myself at a stage when planning and saving for retirement should have been task one, in a position with a company going nowhere, I managed to land a job at a company not only going somewhere, but going somewhere in a hurry, and needing an experienced hand to help accelerate growth. In other words, my own career is proof that a diligent campaign to find a new position while staying employed at a current position can succeed.

As an experienced worker, you are used to a daily routine of getting up and going to work, managing daily and weekly tasks, developing and maintaining relationships with coworkers and (at least generally) enjoying some amount of challenge and stimulation. When that routine is disrupted by suddenly finding yourself out of work, or seeing that likelihood on the horizon, you want to do *something*. While that instinct is correct, it is essential that the something you do be the right thing. Remember that our goals include finding multiple job opportunities and then selecting the one that is best, not simply finding anything and accepting that first opportunity. By customizing this program to your requirements, personality and situation, I believe you will improve the odds.

<u>The First One Hundred Days</u>

The first one hundred days have become the measuring stick for new Presidents of the U.S. (Never mind what might be reasonable to expect of the Chief Executive of the world's sole remaining super power.)

Jonathan Alter wrote a best-selling book that covered Franklin Delano Roosevelt's first one hundred days in office.[4] That period set the standard that the Washington media still uses to assess the performance of all subsequent administrations. At the end of that one hundred day period, television talk shows, newspapers and magazines all reflect on the performance of our new President. Behind the scenes are Presidential transition teams which began work long before the election, developed position papers, identified cabinet candidates and clarified priorities to make those first hundred days as positive and productive as possible. Those teams help the new President get off to as fast and an effective start as possible.

Just like an incoming President prepares intensely with his team before inauguration, you must be thoroughly prepared before you initiate contact. You must resist the urge to start calling and networking before you are ready. Showing up ill-prepared, sending résumés with weak cover letters, or sending inadequately constructed emails or conducting poorly-directed network meetings may squander opportunities to land a position for which you are actually very well suited. Even worse, that can tarnish your reputation.

Once I told a close friend of mine that my firm was looking for a new general counsel. He stated that he knew an outstanding candidate that he had worked with and would strongly support. I met his contact. The meeting that can only be described as painful. Cringe-worthy. That lawyer had worked for the same company for twenty years, had never been in the job market before, and had a résumé that didn't describe accomplishments. He was meeting prospective employers and networking contacts too soon. I certainly wouldn't have hired him, and I was not even comfortable giving him additional network contacts and thereby subjecting my valuable contacts to a bad, time-wasting meeting. He obviously had not spent the appropriate time developing his plan and marketing materials, much less in practicing and perfecting his delivery and answers to likely networking and interview questions.

Spend the appropriate time developing your marketing plan, materials, and prospects and then arrange your supply lines before launching the assault.

Exhibit 7-1 Action Plan

First 100 Days

	Chp.	1+	31+	61+	90+
The planning & preparation phase	2-4				
Develop contact list	5	X			
Create accomplishments list	5	X			
Fitness and appearance program	4	X	X	X	X
Write résumés	6	X			
Design cover letters	15	X	X	X	X
Develop scripts	16	X			
Develop fact lists	6		X		
The targeting phase					
Develop targets	10	X	X	X	X
Research targets	19		X	X	X
The execution phase	18-22				
Post résumés to job web sites	7		X		

Find and join networking groups	14		X	X	X
Financial plan	8, 9	X			
Search firm mailing	15			X	
Target company mailing	10			X	
Networking meetings	14		X	X	X
General company mailings	15			X	
Develop personal website	17			X	
Attend trade and professional association meetings	18	X	X	X	X
Monitor job websites	7		X	X	X
Respond to inquiries	19-20		X	X	X
Interviews	19, 20, 21		X	X	X
Follow-up activities	22			X	X
The post-new position phase	25				X

As you see in Exhibit 7-1 there is much to do. Customize this plan to your personal style, but I strongly recommend against omitting any step; you are simply reducing your chances of success or increasing the time requirement to locate a new position.

Once the seven actions in the planning and preparation phase are completed, you are primed and prepared for an efficient market launch. By this time, you've likely done many or all of them.

In Table 7-2, we present an example weekly calendar with time budgets for each critical job search activity.

Exhibit 7-2

Weekly Job Search Schedule

Time	Mon-Fri	Sat/Sun
6AM	Exercise; Watch Business TV e.g. –CNBC or Bloomberg	
7	Breakfast; read news	
8	Check emails	Check emails
8:15	Begin east coast calls and emails	
9	Calls & emails	Check & respond to job websites
10	Network meetings	Prepare mailings to companies & search firms
11	Network meetings	
12	Lunch	
1	Check emails; begin calls and emails	
2	Network meetings	

3	Target company research	
4-6:30	Check emails; begin emails and West coast calls	
6:30	Correspondence and thank you notes	
7	Post résumés, check & respond to job websites	Check & respond to job websites

It is obvious that this schedule envisions a 14 hour weekday and four or five hours each weekend day. This is completely intentional. If you are serious about getting another job and you are over 50, *this is what it is going to take.* There are no shortcuts, no magic methods. Stick to this plan for four weeks, and you will see and feel the momentum building. Plus, you'll be mentally and physically prepared for you new role, where your fitness and discipline will get you off to an outstanding start.

As you can see in the preceding table, there are some common-sense rules that apply:

·   Make calls to the east coast early in the day, central in the middle and west coast in the afternoon and early evening to maximize available time.
·   Search for jobs, post résumés and review job sites in the evening and on weekends – do not waste precious daytime hours on this activity. This is not to diminish the importance of the Internet in your search– particularly for technology-oriented positions– but the goal is time-efficiency.

You may have noticed that networking is presented as a four hour per day activity. Depending upon your personal experience in job search, what you have read and what you have heard from others, you may find that this is surprisingly low or surprisingly high. Arguably the biggest drawback of networking is the time it takes. Most literature emphasizes networking as the most effective job search technique. There are books devoted to the topic. Generally these books recommend reliance on that method to the point of eliminating other techniques. I strongly disagree: networking is indeed a valuable weapon in our job search arsenal; however, to overcome the market perceptions facing middle-aged job seekers, one must apply leverage across all job search methods. Networking requires a significant time requirement. One must devote adequate time to study the company you plan to visit, develop intelligent and thoughtful questions, and prepare thank-you notes and appropriate follow-up. And, of course, to allow for the travel time required. (Networking is covered in detail in Chapter 14; our goal here is to prepare a daily and weekly time budget that adequately comprehends the time it will consume).

Before moving to the next chapter, spend some time developing your own version of this calendar. Whatever method you use today – a classic Franklin Planner, a Day-Timer, Microsoft Outlook, your smartphone program, a tablet, or a big desk calendar to track your daily, weekly and monthly agenda, integrate this into it–budget your time thoughtfully.

Think back through how companies you have worked for have filled positions like the one you are seeking. Modify the suggested time budget in Exhibit 7-2 by leveraging that knowledge of how job changes take place in your industry. For example, if you are in sales, and you know that you are most likely to learn of the best positions available in your industry at an annual industry conference, then organizing a trip to that conference and setting up appointments with the highest potential employers merits a dedication of hours.

Similarly, if you are in the technology field, you know that jobs are increasingly filled by Internet applicants. You then should increase the number of hours spent on-line, and you may want to take some of those hours and shift them to "normal" nine-to-five business hours from the suggested evening and weekend hours.

<u>Current Job Holders</u>

A special note if you currently hold a position, but know or suspect that you are going to lose it: obviously the previous timetable doesn't work for you.

Some individuals have asked me if they should leave their current position to look for a new position full-time. My view: *absolutely not!*

In your current position, no matter how terrible, you probably have access to some capabilities that will represent incremental costs once you are no longer employed. Those may include:

- Use of a copy machine
- Voice mail
- Cheaper long distance calling
- Inclusion in a health care program
- Paid vacation
- A quieter or more professional environment than your home
- Faxing
- Paid holidays
- A 401(k) plan and match
- Training programs
- Administrative assistance
- Computers on a fast network
- A paycheck!

And most importantly, negotiating power. That is, if a prospective new employer becomes interested, they know they have to pay a market price for your talent. (It won't be so obvious to them that you are anxious to leave your current employer). In the current environment, all too often employers try to take advantage of unemployed candidates and recruit them below market price.

As an employed job seeker, you will have to be far more discerning in creating time for your job search. This doesn't mean not finding time to get that exercise program working. The appearance issues discussed in Chapter 4 are the same. So you'll need to find exercise time either before or after work.

Initially, you may have to rely more heavily on an Internet-based search.

Insider tip: many companies routinely monitor job sites for résumés of current employees. Be sure to take all the steps the site recommends to keep your identity isolated from your current employer.

Insider tip 2: don't store your résumé on your employer's computer:

a)   It might be found,
b)   You might find yourself fired and escorted out of the building with no chance to retrieve it.

Insider tip 3: keep multiple backups of your résumé. Once you've invested the time in preparing a résumé, make sure that you've got a copy on a flash drive, CD, Google Docs, DropBox or use Carbonite or another backup system. There are too many easy choices not to stay backed-up.

Insider tip 4: don't copy your résumé on your employer's copy machine. We all know the stories describing how the boss found the employee's résumé on the copier. And did you know that copiers have memory? Most copiers store an image file of everything copied. (!)

Make every possible effort to attend industry and functional meetings and conventions. Many conventions are known as the place that industry veterans attend to find a new position. Whenever you attend, participate in everything. That is, go to all the sessions from breakfast sessions through cocktail receptions through dinner. Use every opportunity to expand your network and contacts.

Some hiring employers insist on "sitting" candidates, that is, one currently employed. I'm not exactly sure of the rationale–but it can't be ignored. If you are employed but think a change is in the offing, take advantage of your situation to the maximum extent possible (while maintaining integrity–which, in the long run, is a much more important thing to have than a job).

We'll rejoin the topic of finding a new position while getting the most out of an expiring position later.

OK, I can sense that you are eager for action. Only one more preparatory step before you move to the front and get one hundred percent engaged.

Chapter 8 Procurement

"Nine times of ten an army has been destroyed because its supply lines have been severed." General
Douglas MacArthur.

In your last position, you were familiar with the purchasing process at your
employer. Whether it was for office supplies, travel, goods for resale, raw
materials, advertising or a capital item, there was a method. For most of us,
losing a job exposes our financial (in)security; if a transition to new
employment stretches to months or years, the financial strain can be severe.
Now you must act as your own purchasing agent and you must be a smart
one. The savings can be substantial.

Objective: Obtain the goods and services you need for a successful job search
at the lowest possible price.

You are going to be buying a lot of goods and services and need to plan
wisely. Further, you don't want to purchase on a rush basis. Purchases will
include:

- Internet service
- Multiple phone lines
- Printing
- Long distance
- Cellular services
- Office supplies
- Health care

Office Supplies

Get in the wholesale club habit. I go to my nearby wholesale club at least
once per month and buy all our paper products: paper plates and cups, toilet
paper, tissues, and paper towels, along with certain grocery and health
products like vitamins. The savings are substantial. Amazon Prime is a good
alternative.

If you are like me and prefer to look at long documents on paper rather than
on a screen, you are going to print a lot of Security and Exchange Committee
(SEC) documents like 10K's for review, as well as printing résumés, cover

letters, job specifications and the like. Therefore, you will use a forest of trees. You should buy computer paper by the carton. Both the wholesale clubs (Sam's, Costco and BJ's) and the office superstores (Staples, Office Depot, and Office Max) sell paper in multi-ream cartons at significant discounts. Buy trees wholesale.

Check wholesale clubs for all office supplies you need before other outlets: the wholesale clubs typically work on lower margins.

Printing

Buy printing wisely. If you are getting your résumés professionally printed, then be a careful shopper: you can achieve substantial savings on printing. Buy the paper yourself; arrange the printing schedule so that you don't need same day or twenty-four hour turnaround. Printers love rush jobs because they demand a substantial price premium. The same goes for business cards. Again, there are attractive online options for printing and cards such as Vistaprint (www.vistaprint.com) and Moo (us.moo.com)

Long Distance

The market for unlimited minutes for either land or mobile phones is highly competitive. There are multiple ways to purchase calling time effectively. An unlimited calling plan for your mobile or home phone, prepaid calling cards and Skype are all valid options. If you can afford the unlimited plan for your mobile, that is probably the best option. You stay connected as you travel to interviews, networking meetings, or whatever.

Increasingly mobile users consume far more data on their mobile devices than voice usage. And the telcos have responded with a variety of data plans. To minimize overages, take advantage of Wi-Fi connections. Usually, when one is connected via a Wi-Fi network, data charges are not included in monthly usage cost. Perhaps that is why I see so many people with laptops and IPads hanging around Panera restaurants….

Buying Broadband

Shop for Internet suppliers. In most of the U.S. this usually means that you are comparing a duopoly supplier environment: the local cable provider vs. the local phone company. Frequently there are bundled offers with local and long distance service or cable TV. These are worth evaluating. If you are fortunate there may be some Wi-Fi hotspots in your area. Subscription to a Wi-Fi ("air card") service could provide you with a third high-speed choice.

<u>Separate phone line</u>

Unless you absolutely cannot afford it, you must have a separate phone line for your calling and call answering. I might relent somewhat if you have the use of an office and administrative assistance support or a really good outplacement service. If you are looking for work from your home, if is critical. Again, check for bundled offers with cell phones, or cable television.

<u>Absolutely, Positively, Keep Your Health Care</u>

I know from personal experience the cost, and the benefit of health care insurance. If you are reading this and have the opportunity to get coverage from a former employer under COBRA, you simply must take it. I know of nothing else in America that can devastate individual wealth faster and more thoroughly than succumbing to a serious medical condition while uninsured. I would sell my home if necessary to keep medical coverage.

In many situations, employers must permit downsized, outsourced or terminated employees access to employer-supported health plans under COBRA. If you are not eligible for COBRA, in addition to your job search you must run a health care search. Possible sources include health exchanges under The Affordable Health Care Act (aka Obamacare), the various providers of other insurance you might have–such as your current provider of auto, homeowners or life insurance. Many professional organizations and other affinity groups have relationships with insurers and service providers. Start your investigation there.

In summary, you are an experienced worker. Along the way, you have seen your employers waste money buying too much or too little, buying to soon or too late, or buying from the wrong supplier. Leverage that knowledge and be an excellent purchasing agent.

Chapter 9 Budget Cuts

Every year, the various military units submit their budget requests. These add up to hundreds of billions more than the country can afford. So, the generals, admirals and their staffs make cuts. Then the Secretary of Defense makes more cuts. Then the Director of the Office of Management and Budgets makes more cuts. Then, at some point Congress weighs-in.

You have the same task. As severance dries up, unemployment benefits expire and you dip into your precious savings, you must be able to fund a marketing campaign without going bankrupt.

Objective: Preserve your capital while supporting a thoughtful transition.

Here are some tips.

If you have a lot of credit card debt, find a radio station that carries Dave Ramsey and listen to him every day. Check out his website (www.daveramsey.com). He has the best and most practical advice for managing personal credit issues and problems of anyone I'm aware of. And a good philosophy on life as well.

Mortgage

If you have a mortgage, talk to your lender about paying interest-only for a while. If your mortgage is relatively high compared to the value of the home, this won't help much. On the other hand, if you've amortized a lot of the mortgage or made a substantial (say forty percent or more) down payment, this may reduce your monthly obligation a lot.

Contrary to old westerns–and currently popular mythology-banks hate to foreclose on mortgages, and will be more flexible than Gumby to help you, especially if you have a history of paying on time. Contact your bank. And do it early–bankers are most helpful if you tell them that in a few months you might need their help–and less helpful if you are telling them your problems after missing four payments.

Retirement accounts

I am not going to recommend that you draw any of your retirement plans unless it is an act of desperation. But if you have a 401(k), check if you can borrow against it. This preserves plan earnings and doesn't trigger any tax consequences. You can use the funds to keep your medical coverage current, pay for a computer or second phone line. When you return to work, you must budget paying yourself back, and you must follow through on your commitment.

Similarly, if you are regularly contributing to a retirement plan or IRA during a severance period, you may want to consider diverting that to a money market account you can access. As long as you find work and make a contribution during the tax year, you will only be out the earnings your contribution would have created during that time.

<u>Sources of cash</u>

Have bank certificates of deposit, treasury bills, savings bonds or a stock brokerage account? All of these can be used for collateral for borrowing at attractive rates without triggering the tax consequences of an asset sale.

<u>Expense cuts</u>

Become an electricity miser. Almost anyone in the US can reduce his electric bill. I certainly wasn't too concerned about mine until a lengthy unemployment period. Now I'm disciplined about turning off lights, TVs and computers when I leave a room. I've replaced exterior doors with better-insulated ones, added weather stripping and more. My guess is that we've cut our power by 25-30% and not given up a thing. I've even switched some lights to those goofy spiral fluorescents and even bought a couple of those super-expensive LCD lights. There is an endless list of things to do, each of which may save less than one percent of your usage, but collectively make a nice difference.

If you are a smoker, you have an opportunity for giant savings. Time to quit. Cold turkey. Now. In addition to the monetary benefit, you will dramatically improve your odds of getting hired. While the common belief is that women and minorities are disadvantaged in the hiring place, I think that is a bunch of hooey. Overweight people, older people and smokers are discriminated against in the hiring process. As part of this program, first, we reduce the odds of being discriminated against for our age. Second, we get in shape and eliminate being discriminated against for our weight. Now, you must lose the cigarettes. Presto! From target of discrimination to sought after candidate!

Switch to take-out food. If you are like my wife and me, you eat out more than you eat at home. After all, you are older and perhaps your children are grown and gone. I'm not going to tell you to suddenly change that habit, but here are two ideas. First, make a slight downgrade. Trade in The Palm for Outback. When you land the new job, celebrate at The Palm. Second, buy dinner to go and don't buy the beverages. Restaurant folks are smart, they frequently are price sharp on entrées, but more than offset it on beverages. You'll be amazed at the difference in your check. And you save some of the tip. Tip nicely when you land a new job.

<u>Tax deductions</u>

Get your deductions. At this writing, you are entitled to deduct reasonable expenses associated with finding new employment. Keep detailed records of the office supplies you purchase, your long distance calls, mileage and other costs of networking, traveling for interviews, computer supplies, printing expenses and mailing costs. Check with your tax advisor because these rules change all the time. But, if your unemployed period stretches for a while, this can accumulate into a large expense, and a valuable deduction.

Chapter 10 Targets

"Attack him where he is unprepared, appear where you are unexpected."
Sun Tzu, *The Art of War*

How do you identify target companies?   Employ wide-ranging criteria to create the largest possible universe. Then make the list intelligent. Otherwise you might:

- End up working for some dead-end company that eventually peters-out, leaving you back in the job market with interviewers asking "what you could have possibly been thinking to have accepted *that* position". [Think Caldor's, Burger Chef, Packard-Bell, Country-Wide Mortgage, Tower Records.]
- Take a position with an over-leveraged company that requires bankruptcy–and massive layoffs–to cut enough costs to survive-or makes the cuts and still doesn't survive [e.g.-United Airlines, U.S. Airways, Levitz, Lehman Bros., Circuit City, Wachovia].
- Find yourself with a technology laggard such as DEC, Wang, or MySpace.
- Work for some bunch of losers. (It has been hard, but I have resisted the urge to name some of the losers I've worked for.)
- End up working for a bunch of liars: think Enron and WorldCom.

The companies you select as targets must reflect your particular skills, experience and desires.

Self-analysis

First things first: what do you really want to do? If you have had your ideal job somewhere in your work history, then this gets pretty easy. Block out two hours and rehash what made it so great.

Speed of change in the industry?

Intellectual challenge?

Working as part of a great team?

A great leader?

International travel– or home every night?

Family friendly or incredibly demanding?

Growth rates on the edge of chaos? Or meticulously controlled stability?

Friendly coworkers? Or solitary contemplation?

Freedom of action–in control of your time and direction?

Great on-the-job learning opportunities?

Recognition for your contribution?

A reputation for excellence in your area of technical expertise?

A prestigious employer?

Wild-eyed creative types– or disciplined professionals?

Small town environment– or big city hustle and bustle?

If you land on the interstice of fortune and skill, you may get an opportunity to work for a company you target. Make no mistake–it isn't easy and it doesn't always work. But this analysis is a key building block in landing that next position. As you work towards your target company, you are going to meet dozens, hundreds and perhaps thousands of people who can help you find a new position. I personally have never targeted a company and landed a position at my target. However, I know individuals who have, and enough of them, to believe that the attempt merits devoting some of your precious hours.

Objective: Land a Position at an Employer You Choose

Tactic one: describe the ideal opportunity. Once you've completed your self-analysis, create a one-sentence description of your ideal target. You will share this ideal with all the contacts you make. "I'm looking for an opportunity in a stable, profitable health care or closely related company, where I can continue to develop my capabilities for obtaining the best reimbursement of medical costs for patients." Or, "I really had a blast working with the engineers at Raytheon; I'd like an opportunity in an engineering management role with a major defense contractor in the missile defense area."

Sharing these statements will help your contacts quickly determine whether they can help you. These one-sentence summaries are not fuzzy; people will instantly know if they have an idea and a connection for you.

Tactic two: identify broad targets. This is most likely a library activity. Almost every business and trade industry periodical publishes an annual industry ranking, generally by revenue, but frequently sorted many other ways as well, such as by profits, growth rates or returns. For example, the *Fortune 500* issue is sorted several ways – revenues, profits, assets, stockholders' equity and more. It also shows how many of the 500 are located in each state–and which cities have the most *Fortune 500* headquarters. It also shows performance of the largest companies by industry group. The Forbes 1000 similarly has numerous slices of the data, with the obvious difference of more companies.

Outside of these corporate giants tracked by the general business press, industry trade periodicals go into detail for an industry. For example *Furniture Today* has the Furniture 100. Very few of the companies in the Furniture 100 make the *Forbes* or *Fortune* lists, but if you are interested in staying in the furniture field, this is a great, quick way to turn up some names for further analysis. It is very unlikely that you have chosen a field that doesn't have a trade publication ranking your industry.

Tactic three: create logical screens. Let's say that your ideal job is in the restaurant industry, in a regional management role with a fast growing chain restaurant company, with heavy involvement in new markets and opening new locations. Use *Restaurant Business*'s list of the biggest chains and *Inc*'s list of the fastest growing companies to identify those companies growing fast that have enough strength to keep the momentum.

In Chapter 14 we'll describe the perfect network call to make to get maximum help in identifying those companies that most closely match your ideal position, and in Chapter 19 you will learn how to deeply research the companies that you find most interesting.

Let's call the companies you have listed as Group One.

Tactic four: always have a "Plan B". Now you've created a targeted list for your ideal job. But you just might find that in this economy your ideal targets just don't have an immediate opportunity. So, what was the first runner up? Do this same exercise for the next best job. There are lots of reasons one can get depressed in a job search. By having a back-up plan we can avoid this potential downer. That is, if ideal targets in your Group One don't pan out, you are ready to go to ideal Group Two. And, the contacts you've made in Group One are still out there and may turn up something for you while you are tackling Group Two.

If you are a) more flexible about your next position, b) qualified for a variety of roles, and c) more concerned about finding a position in particular areas than in a particular company or industry, then identifying businesses in a geographical market may be a better first step. See Chapter 5 on the Business Journals.

Chapter 11 Propaganda

Propaganda: information, ideas or rumors deliberately spread to help or hurt a person, cause, movement, group, etc.

The more people who have a favorable impression of you, the faster you're going to connect with a new opportunity. Companies and individuals track their Internet "hits", page views, time on site, unique visitors, etc. to determine how well that site is attracting viewership. In advertising, agencies track "gross rating points" to determine how many impressions of their client are hitting prospective customers. Agencies know that it takes a lot of impressions to build brand awareness. Similarly, in your search for a new job, you need to generate rating point –favorable impressions–fast, and in the highest volume that you can. Big networks win.

<u>Propaganda part 1: publicity</u>

Now that our direct assaults have been launched, it is time to augment them with a series of publicity efforts that will promote you to the market. Key opportunities include:

- Letters to editors.
- Public speaking.
- Association meeting.
- Blogs.
- Facebook.
- Twitter.

<u>Letters to Editors</u>

Since you are a mature, experienced and talented individual, you have technical knowledge and expertise. As I noted in earlier chapters, essentially every industry has magazines, newsletters and websites devoted to it. Many of those publications also host industry events and conferences. Scan the magazines and web sites covering the industries that you know best, find a topic of interest that you can comment on and send a letter to the editor. While some magazines get thousands of responses, others see only a few. There is no downside to this effort: if you get published your name is sent to thousands, and perhaps millions, of readers. If not, scanning industry and trade periodicals keeps you current on trends and developments. Having fresh, topical knowledge is always valuable in an interview.

<u>Public speaking opportunities</u>

The benefits of accepting public speaking opportunities are almost limitless:

· Many associations struggle to get speakers; if you help them out as a last minute substitute, you've earned the gratitude of a meeting chairman.
· It keeps your speaking and presentation skills polished.
· Preparation for your presentation keeps your industry or technical knowledge sharp.

If you are well-known in your industry or have been a consistent participant in a technical specialty area, let it be known to association presidents or meeting chairmen that you are available for speaking opportunities. Needless to say, if you get that opportunity, you must make a terrific presentation, creating a group of excited people talking about you the next day. In essence, they become your personal sales force! (The rules for personal appearance checking from Chapter 4 also apply here).

Insider tip: let it be known your speech that copies of your presentation, PowerPoint charts, etc. will be made available. Get a business card and an email address from everyone who asks for a copy and send it to them by email. Make sure the cover of your speech or your title slide and final slide have your name and contact information. Build your network!

Insider tip two: the Internet really has changed everything. Dance competitions are far more challenging because dancers see the best in the world on YouTube. Public speaking and presentations have gotten far better due to Ted Talks. There are now thousands of Ted Talk presentations on YouTube. Some have been viewed millions of times. Watch a few to get pointers and to observe some of the techniques of the world's best presenters. Incorporate them into your presentations.

<u>Association meetings and Trade Shows and Conferences</u>

Just because you are not the keynote speaker at association meetings doesn't mean you shouldn't be dependable member and a regular at meetings. I'm a member of the Financial Executives Institute, and try to make every meeting when I'm in town. An industry that I was once in, residential furniture, has two large selling events each year: the spring and fall furniture markets. When I was employed in that industry, I attended those regularly. National tradeshows offer unrivaled networking opportunities.

If there is a hot new topic in your industry, it may provide you with a unique opportunity for powerful image making and public relations, and may lead to at least some revenue-generating assignments. As of this writing, multiple topics are consuming boards of directors and financial executives including: compliance with the myriad new rules emanating from new legislation ("Dodd-Frank" bill), from the Securities and Exchange Commission and the stock exchanges with new regulations, and from the bodies governing public accounting. Topics such as "accounting convergence"-the project to make uniform financial reporting rules internationally, rules for "uncertain" tax positions, the emotional topic of tax "inversions" are top of mind for many. Hundreds, perhaps thousands, of lawyers, insurance brokers and CPAs are publishing and speaking on those topics, generating tremendous publicity for themselves and their firms. Similarly, how much resource businesses should devote to social media, and how to use it most effectively, is a lively topic in marketing and other circles. What are the current issues in your field? Those topics are likely subjects for questions in an interview, likely areas for dinner table conversation association meetings, and present the best opportunity for you to generate some favorable industry propaganda.

Trade shows offer the same opportunities–but with a slightly different twist. Most association meetings have a strong education or training component. At trade shows, sales lead generation and actual selling are the order of the day. So contacts must be made in a way that doesn't interfere with commerce. If you prevent a transaction from happening you certainly aren't advancing your career opportunity. Therefore, at a trade show, you must concentrate your efforts at a time of the day, and in a way that you don't alienate the people you are interested in (see "Targeted Networking" below). Don't act like a customer and waste some salesperson's time! There are always programs, dinners, breakout sessions, award banquets and the like at trade shows. Those provide the time and place to network.

Most trade shows now have Twitter hash tags and TweetUps. Make sure that you take advantage of both. Smart, hip Tweeting live from general sessions or important talks can build your reputation and following very rapidly.

When attending any meeting or conference, make sure to have an ample supply of business cards. It should go without saying, but I'm saying it anyway, your card must contain both your cell phone number and your email address. While titles aren't necessary on your card, if you are somewhat uncomfortable with a card with no title, try "Consultant" or one of my personal favorites "Investments". You should also have a few crisp new résumés copies (not folded) in a small valise with you.

And, again as always, follow-up promptly on any contact you made.

Blogs

While chat rooms, message boards and blogs must be used judiciously, there may be personal propaganda opportunities here as well. Look for industry or technical specialty groups that you can join in. Don't post too often and obey the mores of the chat group. When you post, be thoughtful and take the time for good grammar and spelling. (Chat rooms can also be an excellent source of rumors and gossip on potential employers. Message boards on high volume sites like Yahoo are the first place to check for lively company gossip).

Remember though, the Internet is Forever. Once you've put it out there, it is there forever. Don't make an Anthony Weiner out of yourself.

Demonstrations

Is your line of work more hands-on or skilled? Look for opportunities to demonstrate. Home Depot and Lowes offer workshops on a variety of home improvement projects such as hanging drywall, installing flooring, and faux painting. Computer user groups demo software techniques. Bass Pro Shops has a mind-boggling list of workshops from fly-fishing to field-dressing a deer to using your turkey-fryer. Skilled practitioners are always in demand.

<u>Propaganda – part 2: résumé techniques</u>

You should never lie on your résumé. The downside of getting caught is far worse than the benefits that you can achieve. (Run this Google search: "five big-shots who lied on their résumé. That's what can happen. However, sticking to the facts doesn't mean that you can't spin events to your advantage.

Ever watch any political debates and in particular the Presidential debates? And then watched the talking head commentary after the debates? Have you noticed how the *all* the campaign managers claim their candidate won? They spin the results as necessary to show the skill, caring, thoughtfulness, daring, mental toughness, etc. of their candidate. Spin is what you must do too.

Here are three propaganda techniques for you to consider. Use any, all or none of them as you see fit.

First, as shown on Exhibit 11-1, is the alternative résumé, which I've called a Career Summary. This résumé presents skills and accomplishments without the chronology dearly loved by executive recruiters. (Recruiters are as lazy as the next person; most of the career summaries they present to employers use a chronological format instead of something that is more insightful–and time-consuming to prepare. They prefer that you do the work with a detailed chronological résumé. Accordingly, Career Summary format should never go to a search firm, or be entered on a search firm site).

This format has the obvious advantage of eliminating those pesky years that show you just how old you really are. (Of course, by the time you've gotten to this chapter you are now leaner and healthier-looking.)

Take some time and design a Career Summary. Repurpose your accomplishments as the core. Then circulate it to your advisors and ask them to give you their thoughts on which of your résumés to use and when. This format is not for everyone, and will strike some potential interviewers as too avant-garde. However, if it succeeds in getting you in the door, you have attained your objective! If they ask numerous questions so that they can take your career achievements format and annotate it into a traditional résumé, then that is just fine–you are there to help them do it, and the non-traditional format didn't keep you from getting the interview. Still, use this format with caution. Every time you need to supply a résumé, take a little time to decide which format has the best chance of getting you an interview with that particular firm or person.

The second technique is to spark up your personal characteristics section with your most physically active sports. In Chapter 3 we started the basic training program. Now you need to add an active lifestyle sport to spiff-up your résumé. Remember, we aren't going to lie on our résumé, so you *must* participate in the sport you include. And it may be a problem on your current budget, so use this technique only if appropriate. But, rock climbing, snow-boarding, mountain biking, marathon running, in-line skating, racquetball, handball, mixed martial arts, wind-surfing, spinning, CrossFit, or power-lifting will put you in a different grouping in the interviewer's mind. Not only as someone participating in demanding physical tests, but someone who is a risk taker. Obviously not some desk-bound old fogey with a spare tire. You reduce the risk that the résumé reader, who hasn't ever seen or met you, guesses that you are wrinkled and pudgy. Rather, you are an action-oriented high-performer.

The third technique is pure propaganda and risky. Summarize that early career experience–while it was valuable, does your next position really depend on that McDonald's job? -into a two sentence statement. If you have multiple degrees–put the year of the last one only. Yes it is obvious. Yes they can easily find out. But *they won't ask*–it is way too dangerously close to (illegal) age discrimination. Remember, the goal of your résumé is to obtain a face-to-face interview. Once you are in the door, your experience and preparation for the interview will carry you. Use this technique only after careful consideration–many career management experts think this approach is a really bad idea.

As always, we are going to use computer power to accelerate this process. As covered in Chapter 5 on information dissemination, Microsoft has helped us by including templates in Microsoft Word. To get a functional format, I went the web (http://office.microsoft.com/templates, then clicked on "Your Career"). I chose the "Minimalist Theme" from a wide variety of templates. As with the templates in Chapter 5, the one change I made was to the font size. I found the font too small. We certainly want it to be easy for the reader to find and read all our information. That then is what we will use to speed our way to a very different format.

Exhibit 11-1

Scott Kreger

Career Summary

2005 Central Ave
Nashville TN 37001
Phone (123) 123-1234; Cell (123) 123-1234; email scott@scottkreger.com

Objective: Join a growing consumer goods company where my extensive experience at the executive level in brand-building and sales generation can make an immediate contribution to revenue and earnings

Key skills and accomplishments

Skill: Driving consumer product sales.

Example of results: Developed entire marketing concept and strategy for new shampoo and conditioner, including approving packaging and point of sale design, driving advertising, consumer and trade promotion. Captured 7% of the US market in the first year, increasing to 9% in the second. Achieved similar share gain in European and Latin American markets. Product line profitability targets were exceeded, with earlier than planned profits in 15th month.

Skill: Managing advertising for effectiveness

Example of results: Assumed responsibility for $30 mil advertising and promotion budget for high-end ladies' apparel chain. Conducted search for new agency, redirected larger part of budget to in-store promotion, changed media mix. Reversed 2% negative same store sales trend to 4% positive trend, while cutting spending by $2 mil.

Skill: Finding new market opportunities

Example of results: For a multinational consumer products company, conducted detailed market research for opportunities for men's fragrance and skin care products. Drove product development process to create new designer lines aimed at young men with growing incomes. Product was introduced in three of US' four largest upscale department stores with all customers displaying full assortments. In this highly volatile market, this product is still holding market share.

Skill: Cost conscious marketing management.

Example of results: For major, multinational PC OEM, maintained constant dollar marketing and advertising budget (declining from 2% of sales to .5%) while revenue grew an average of 30% per year.

Previous positions

Executive Vice President for a national women's designer-oriented apparel company

Vice-President of Marketing for a large PC OEM

Senior Vice President of Marketing and Advertising for a multinational consumer products company

Director of a large strategy consulting firm

Education

MBA Northwestern University 1983

Other interests

Mountain biking, ocean kayaking and reading

As you can see, it is a tightly focused document, designed to highlight experience and results.

Now that you've completed all the preparation, expanded your network and become energized, it's time to get ready for meetings.

Chapter 12 Interrogation

"Be watchful and circumspect in all your movements." General Robert E. Lee

In the course of finding a new job, you will find yourself in many situations that require smooth, crisp answers to tricky, difficult questions. The art is to rehearse the answers until they don't sound rehearsed. Guy Kawasaki, in his excellent *The ART of the START*, states that, for a presentation to be really good, it must be rehearsed 25 times. By the 25th, it will sound natural.

Those situations will occur as you meet with:

- Individuals that you meet networking;
- Attendees at networking group meetings;
- Contacts made at conferences, trade and professional association meetings,
- Recruiters, and
- Managers of hiring companies.

Each of them will ask questions to qualify you. Recruiters and managers will qualify you as a candidate. Individuals you meet during networking will qualify you as worthy of a referral–or not. Hiring authorities will assess your skills and capabilities.

In our litigious society, hiring managers know that previous employers are highly reluctant to give honest information on a previous employee. This concern is heightened when the employee is older and a potential risk for an age discrimination claim. Prior employers will be particularly reticent to comment when an employee was let go for real or perceived performance issues. You may have been let go for a performance issue. Or just another one of millions of Americans caught in a downsizing, or who watched their positions be outsourced, or were in a job reduction program after a merger or acquisition. Or perhaps you had the unfortunate experience of working for a business that filed for bankruptcy. Whatever the cause, you must have a smooth, satisfactory answer for what happened in your last job. If you had a series of positions in the last few years (I know I have!) it is even more imperative that you have a facile, disarming response to the question "why did you leave your last position?" [1]

Objective: Deliver a thorough but concise, natural-sounding answer to an interviewer's toughest questions.

Tactic one: Practice answers to each question. This is most effective if the answers are practiced aloud.

Tactic two: Video yourself answering the questions. If you don't have a video camera, someone you know does. Your smart phone may be able to do it. It is the only way to study your responses, the quality of your voice, and what your eyes and hands are doing while you are dealing with the questions that make you uncomfortable. If I seem to over-emphasize this tactic, it's probably because being filmed was valuable for me personally. I got fired from a terrific, very high-paying, prestigious position. I felt then–and still feel today–that I was doing a great job for that company. As a result, when questioned about why I was terminated, my body language as revealed on video, showed my disappointment, embarrassment and overall unhappiness at getting fired. Whatever my feelings, I had to create a more upbeat response to the question.

Let's look at each situation where you might face tough questioning.

<u>Networking group sessions</u>

Meeting with others who are also looking for a new job can be a very uplifting event. While this sounds very counter-intuitive, seeing others in the same shape you are, and learning of their travails and successes forces the realization that you haven't been singled out by a fickle fate. Properly organized networking sessions provide an opportunities to learn of particular opportunities, to help get doors open, to obtain an objective review of your résumés, cover letters and other marketing materials as well as to practice answering questions. All in a safe, non-threatening atmosphere.

Before you attend a networking session, practice your "elevator speech". You know, that commercial about you that describes your skills and background, and what kind of position you are looking for, that you can deliver while on an elevator ride. Use the networking sessions to polish that critical little sound bite to a shine.

Second, once you've developed and practiced your answer to the question: "What happened in your last position?" on tape, you need to practice it on a real live person. Network meetings makes that easy.

<u>Conferences and Trade Shows</u>

This is speculation on my part, but I'll bet that as much as twenty percent of the people at many a trade shows or conventions are actively looking for work or hoping to make a change. Overcome your reluctance to mingle; the person you walk up to might just as uncomfortable, wants to be in a conversation not standing alone, and in need of a new position, just like you.

As mentioned in prior chapters, most trade shows have cocktail events, breakfasts, luncheons and dinners, and you should attend as many as possible. And you must seek out different individuals at all the sessions to maximize your contacts. Here the question will be "Who do you work for?" Your response needs to be brief and smooth. "I'm in transition" or "I'm looking for a new opportunity", followed by a clear and concise definition of the kind of position you are seeking. "I'm an expert at developing new international markets for consumer product companies; I'm looking for a company that wants to enter the Asian or European market." Or, "I'm known for advanced metallurgy, particularly in industrial manufacturing applications, and I'm looking for companies that need to make products lighter, stronger or more durable." These answers might receive a friendly, if someone distant, response. However, the curious attendee may want to know more about that field. And, if you've targeted the trade show correctly, he may know a lot about that field, and perhaps even a company with a need.

<u>One-on-one Network meetings</u>

In a network meeting, a couple of things can happen. First, the person who has agreed to meet with you is courteous and non-committal and is simply biding time until the meeting is over, when they can breathe a sigh of relief and get back to work. Or, they can size you up and decide if they are willing to invest their precious reputation with others giving you the names and helping you contact others (Networking is extensively covered in Chapter

14).

Assume the best about people. Believe that they sincerely plan to help you, and therefore you must have great answers to questions to help them assess your skills and to think about possible matches. These questions likely will include:

- What kind of position are you looking for?
- What happened in your last position?
- Are you willing to relocate? Where?
- How have you approached your search?
- Are there specific industries you prefer? How did you conclude that those are the appropriate industries?
- Are you considering temporary or interim positions?
- Who else have you meet with?
- What would you like me to do to help you?

<u>The recruiter phone call</u>

Because recruiters can play such a critical role in many job changes, I devote a section later to meetings with recruiters. Hence, for the moment we will restrict ourselves to how to deal with the first call from a recruiter. Since a call from a recruiter–especially for a retained search–means there is a real job out there and a real hiring agent anxious to hire someone, these calls must be handled flawlessly.

First, insure your workspace is organized so that you can retrieve your résumé, list of accomplishments, facts lists and calendar within seconds. When the call comes in, put the recruiter on hold briefly to make sure those items are open and available for you. Second, stand up while talking. This opens up your diaphragm, and creates more confidence in your voice.

Over the years, essentially all of my job changes have come with the assistance of a recruiter who had a position to fill. At this writing, however, the recruiting industry is still slowly emerging from the worst recession it has ever experienced. While a recruiter was involved in my last job change, the company, not the recruiter, found me, and, in essence, he was just a step in the interview process. In the current market, companies are using technology, especially LinkedIn to find excellent candidates without the expense of a recruiter.[2]

Nonetheless, most of the very best, highest paying positions, and many of the better positions, are filled with the assistance of a search firm.

Historically, recruiters used a very straightforward process to identity and interview candidates. An associate, frequently fresh out of business school, studied the recruiter's existing data base of candidates. Depending upon the size of the recruiting firm, the data base could be extensive. The analyst augmented that list with names from LinkedIn. The analyst began calling names culled from the database, learning about the industry and key players as she goes. For a senior position, a quality search firm will talk to about 200 people. At each call, the analyst probes skills, interest, and match with the job specification, as well as trying to identify other potential candidates. (If you've never been contacted by a retained executive search firm, the pitch is simple: "I have been retained to fill a senior position with a (rapidly-growing/industry leading/well-known) client. Your name has come up as an expert in this area. In your current position you might not find this of interest, but you might know someone I should talk to." Of course, if you are a strong candidate, they do indeed hope that *you* are interested)

After the associate has screened a couple of hundred people, they will recommend 10-15 for the senior recruiter to talk to. After a thorough phone screen, the senior recruiter will select 7-8 to meet in person (or, in today's more cost controlled situation, a video conference).

The recruiter will then select 4-5 to present to his client.

That approach is still used by some of the surviving large recruiting firms. However, with the power of the Internet and the glut of highly-qualified unemployed or underemployed candidates, recruiters nowadays frequently post positions on Career Builder or Monster, quickly sort through the thousands of responses, and start contacting the individuals that match the search criteria most closely. (Reminder: we covered including keywords in your documents in Chapter 6).

There are no real standards for recruiters. Anyone can be one by sending an announcement, having a phone number and an email address and printing some business cards. (Really, today with web pages and the Internet, you can even skip the business card step.) While there are some highly skilled professionals in the field there are also some real hopeless masqueraders. Nonetheless, always prepare assuming that the recruiter is highly skilled.

If you get that recruiter call, you must navigate the whitewater of questions to get the chance to visit the hiring company.

Typical recruiter questions include:

1. The well-worn, "I have your résumé but tell me about yourself in your own words."

2. Questions to get a firm grip on size of staff, number of direct reports, and dollars and/or of responsibility you managed. (If you have only worked in small companies, but he has a search for a multi-billion business, he will likely rule you out based on the size of the budget or number of people you have managed, unless you have experience in both large and smaller companies). Examples would be:

    a. What is the largest budget you've managed?
    b. What were the revenue and profits under your management?
    c. What was the amount of the assets under your management?
    d. In your last position, how many people reported directly to you? What were their titles?
    e. How much did sales grow under your leadership?
    f. Specifically, how much cost and how many people did you take out of the organization?
    g. What software and operating systems did you employ?
    h. How many others worked in the laboratory with you?
    i. How was your bonus determined?

3. The more discerning, "Describe a situation in which you were very effective".

4. Describe your management style. [5]

5. Name some key mistakes you have made.

6. (If you are like me, and have too many positions on your résumé), "Why you weren't able to stay in one place longer?"

7. What happened in your last position?[6]

8. Describe your strengths? Weaknesses?

9. In what kind of business culture are you most effective?

10. What would your former boss say about you?

11. What would (insert the name of a co-worker) say about you?

12. What would (insert the name of a subordinate) say about you?

For each of these questions that are pertinent to you, you must have smooth, practiced answer. It shows that you are prepared, in control of your facts, and able to respond easily in a situation with a certain amount of tension. Your accomplishments from Chapter 5 should make developing responses to these questions easy.

Here are your objectives as you are interrogated by a recruiter.

<u>Determine your interest in the position</u>

Determine if you have a real interest in the position. No matter how gloomy your job prospects seem, don't pursue a job that you aren't sincerely interested in–you might well get it. That will prove to be worse to both your psyche and your career management. And not just in the long run, but perhaps even in near term.

<u>Determine your qualifications</u>

Decide if you really are very well qualified. You don't want to be in way over your head; that is a certain doom loop. Conversely, if you can do this in your sleep and know that it will bore you to the brink of suicide, pass it up.

Be realistic. If this position calls for someone who can do gymnastics on water, and you can merely walk on water, better to find out now than to take it and fail.

<u>Understand the culture</u>

Ask a lot about the culture. Life is too short to work somewhere you aren't going to fit and succeed. If you are used to, and feel best in a disciplined, structured business, and this position is with a chaotic, continually on the brink business, it might not be in your best interest to try. *Cultural fit is frequently a better indicator of success than other qualifications.*

<u>Gauge the recruiter's interest in your candidacy</u>

If you sense a subtle shift in the tone and tenor of the questions and discussions, from quizzing you about your skills, accomplishments, background, compensation and education, to asking you about your willingness to relocate, the recruiter is considering you a potential candidate. If he then begins to fill you in on some details of the company and the individual who the opening reports to, then he is considering you for his presentation list. At this point, you must ask the recruiter your most important questions. At a minimum, these include:

Why weren't there good internal candidates?

How have others hired from the outside done compared to internal promotions?

How did you get this search? This is a critically important question. If the recruiter has placed several people within the firm, she knows a lot about the company and the decision makers, and therefore is a very valuable source of information on the business.

What process will the company use to make a decision, and what is the timetable? Again, another question that should provide valuable insight into: who the real decision makers are, how fast or deliberate they like to be in making a decision, and whether they are likely to use a consensus-building or top-down approach.

<u>Build a positive relationship with the recruiter</u>

You want to cultivate a relationship with the search executive. If you aren't a fit, say so, but commit to come up with a reference for him if you possibly can. If you supply a great candidate, your stock rises with the search executive, and you'll likely hear from him again.

Insider tip 1. When the associate calls for a position that you haven't applied for digitally, ask for a job specification. Read it carefully, making notes about how you match and don't match the qualifications. This will help you prepare for the questions from the recruiter.

Insider tip 2. Keep a file either on paper or digitally that you can retrieve very rapidly of jobs you have applied for online. That file must contain the position description or job specification that was posted, your email response, and any custom cover letter or résumés that you provided. Never rely on your memory for specifics, remember that you are contacting thousands!

As we covered, if you are dealing with one of the major firms (see list on Exhibit 12-1), the process almost always begins with a call from an associate, or research analyst who is trying to identify the players in the industry, build the initial list of names, and highlight a preliminary list of candidates. If you scored well with the analyst, he will call back to set up a second round of discussions the senior recruiter who actually has the search and the responsibility to see that it gets filled successfully. You may then get a call from that recruiter for a second round of vetting. This may be followed by:

- An in-person interview with the recruiter
- A meeting with the client
- A video conference with the recruiter.

In the increasingly digital world, with skyrocketing travel costs, recruiters are increasingly using video conferencing to conduct second round interviews. You should eagerly accept the offer of a video interview. If you have the choice between an in-person interview and a video interview <u>take the video conference!</u>

Why? First, the video conference saves enormous travel time that you can put to far better use networking and making additional contacts.

Second, in a video conference, you have a table.

A table, you say? Yep.

Insider tip: If the video conference is to be held at a facility, arrive a few minutes early. Have them show you the controls for the equipment (if you can use a computer game joystick, you can use video conference gear). Set the camera to show you from, say, the middle of your chest up – so that the table isn't in view. Once you have that mastered, organize all your key materials in front of you: your résumé, your accomplishments list and your fact sheets. You should be able to glance down at any of them to refresh your memory with the facts, accomplishments and other information on your materials quickly. Without missing a beat. (Of course, you mustn't pick up the papers, rustle them or generally give away that you have crib sheets–or worse, distract your audience).

Insider tip 2: Similarly, if you will be using Skype, arrange the area that will be seen on-camera just like a television news set. Make sure the background isn't distracting and the light is flattering.

And there is a third reason.

Insider tip 3: In a video conference, you get to wear make-up. The women readers of course were already planning to wear make-up. For women, take a little extra time for make-up. For men, this is your chance to take a few years off. I have a brown spot on a cheek. What the old folks used to call a "liver spot". Clearly, it has appeared with age. Too much sun or whatever. But when I have video interviews and meetings, that rascal just isn't there. I'm not saying that men should do the full Hollywood leading man treatment, but I do strongly recommend that you cover up big old pimples, places that you've had skin lesions removed and the like. Video conference equipment isn't typically hi-def after-all. Take advantage of this excellent propaganda opportunity.

If you have an in-person interview with the recruiter, remember our insider tip about arriving early and allowing adequate time to check out your appearance.

Exhibit 12-1

Largest Retained Search Firms

Korn Ferry
Russell Reynolds
Heidrich & Struggles
Spencer Stuart
Spherion
Hudson Highland Group
Christian & Timbers
DHR International
Egon Zehnder
A.T. Kearney
Battalia Winston
AMROP/Hever Group
Boyden
Stanton Chase
Michael Page
Solomon Page
Norman Broadbent
Allen & Assoc.
The Witney Group
TMP Worldwide
Herbert Mines
Lucas Group
Whitehead Mann
The Lancer Group
NGS Global

Chapter 13 Home Base

After your daily regimen of exercise, mailing, calling and networking, comes daily housework. "Housework", you may ask. "Why?" First, many of your days searching for a new position will be frustrating, disappointing and unfulfilling. You need a sense of accomplishment-we all do. Second, the odds are high that your next position will require relocating. This combination creates both the need and the opportunity to perform a series of actions to maintain and improve your home base. These activities should build some economic value while providing you some endorphins from getting results that your work used to provide.

As you read this, you may have been out of work for months. In the current job market, taking six months to eighteen months to find a new position isn't unusual. My last transition took nine months. Do not underestimate the possibility of getting not just discouraged, but really depressed as this process drags on. There will be days when picking up the phone to make cold calls is simply too humiliating to face. Waiting for the promised returned phone call becomes too frustrating. Having some tasks scheduled diverts your mind from your search, and provides important psychic rewards when completed.

Professor Teresa Amabile of Harvard along with Steven Krosner, completed a multiyear analysis of worker satisfaction and motivation. Their conclusion? Progress towards results was the best motivation-better than rewards, recognition, etc.[7]

When was the last time you relocated? While the average American moves every four years, the distribution around the mean is broad. If you have been in your current residence for a while, preparation for relocation may be significant, and as a result even more important. This is further exacerbated by the lingering effect of the Great Recession that causes houses to be on the market far longer than in any phase of prior business cycles going back decades.

My recommendation is that every Monday you prepare the list of six maintenance items for the week – one per day, and then one larger task. The first five must be things that can be accomplished either before or after regular business hours. Save the larger task for the weekend.

The goals:

- Prepare for relocation.
- Get the sense of accomplishment that used to come from your job.
- Get more than caught-up; get ahead so that you start your new position without the weight of deferred home projects.
- Create a highly-effective work environment
- Add value to your home. That might just become important for several reasons.

I'll admit to getting psychic income when I complete a task. Checking off a to-do list gives me a little boost. I don't just have a day-planner action list at work. I make a separate list for weekends and love marking items complete. You too may be missing that sense of achievement or progress. Tackle some of the following tasks and see if your spirits are lifted.

Tactics: Exhibit 13-1 presents a thought-starter list. The potential list is unlimited and must be customized to your personal situation.

Exhibit 13-1 Base Camp Maintenance

<u>Exterior</u>

Fertilize lawn, shrubs and trees.
Plant seasonal color
Weed
Seed
Patch concrete or asphalt
Touch-up paint
Stain or seal deck
Clean gutters
Spray for insects
Trim shrubs
Prune trees
Rake leaves
Mulch beds

<u>Garage and store rooms</u>

Clean-up, throw out
Perform maintenance on engines (mowers, edgers, blowers, string trimmers, etc.).
Sharpen tools
Organize tools
Remove grease and stains from floors
Install peg board or slot wall

<u>Interior</u>

Clean out every closet
Organize dresser drawers
Organize kitchen drawers
Organize kitchen cabinets
Organize pantry
Clean out refrigerator.
Touch-up paint

Patch plaster or wallboard
Remove carpet stains
Change furnace and air-conditioning filters
Oil squeaky doors
Prepare list of selling features for your home
Conduct a garage or EBay sale of all that excess stuff you've accumulated.
Organize computer files, directories, flash drives, DVD's and CD's
Organize all those videos and pictures you have stacked up.
Get your tax records together.
Dig out any info on your apartment lease or home mortgage. Get it ship shape.
Organize all your insurance policies
Donate all the excess you've created to charity. There are people who really need what is excess to you.

Automobiles

Wash 'em, wax 'em.
Check tire pressure and rotate tires.
Change the oil.
Perform scheduled maintenance.
Clean out the glove box and console.

Don't underestimate the benefits of this effort: here are some possible effects of adding base camp maintenance to your daily program:

- You may find an employer who is in a critical need and wants you to start *immediately*. Having this behind you makes you more mobile and flexible-characteristics that you want to be known for.
- You will add value to your home.
- Someone who needs help will benefit from your gifts.
- Further, some psychiatrists have commented on the emotional benefits of getting rid of unnecessary stuff to enable a better focus on the important things and people in your life.
- Getting these things done gives you an important sense of job satisfaction.
- It helps reestablish a routine.

·   It shows your spouse that you are doing everything you can, not only to find a new position, but to do your share while your income is reduced.

<u>Creating a highly-effective environment</u>

Whether you have an outplacement office, a home office or are conducting a job search from your kitchen table, you need an efficient environment. Most people are more effective when distractions are minimized.

There are several things you need to have within reach:

- · Cellphone
- · Résumé
- · Computer
- · Calendar
- · Something for note-taking
- · Talking points/accomplishment list

Use after hours and weekend time to eliminate attention-grabbers. Typically that means organizing your files on active prospects and research on target employers where they can be quickly accessed. A clean work surface is almost always an advantage. Items stacked around are silently campaigning for your attention.

Of course, there are equally distracting digital time wasters. Twitter, Facebook, and LinkedIn can be powerful tools for finding a new position. But they can also suck-up valuable time better spent networking. I recommend that you don't set your computer or smartphone to notify you of new email, Tweets or Facebook posts. Concentrate on the task at hand.

Grab some endorphins by completing some tasks.

In the next chapter we get serious about building your larger network by networking.

Chapter 14 Networking

"Perpetual optimism is a force multiplier". General Colin S. Powell.

If there is one constant theme to this book it is that larger networks win. The larger the number of your connections, and the stronger their commitment, the better the odds that you will land that next spot.

Next to books on how to improve your résumé, the most popular topic about landing a new job is networking. Everyone has a view of: a) what a tremendous percentage of jobs are found through networking; b) how to be a more effective networker; and c) what is in it for the folks who volunteer a part of their critical workday for a meeting. Many of those books, as well as many career coaches and experts expound the concept that, particularly for higher-paying positions, networking is the only realistic way to find a position. My view is somewhat different: networking is an important weapon in your battle for a new position, but it is by no means the only weapon, so it must be used appropriately.

Networking Objectives:

- Discover job opportunities.
- Employ geometric math to expand your network.
- Get an increasing number of potential hiring managers who know you, remember your name and have a favorable impression of you.

Tactics:

Meet as many people as possible *and practical* to learn of opportunities.

Networking *is* essential to finding your next position. It can also be demeaning, difficult, humiliating and humbling. But it frequently can also be rewarding. There are two critical drawbacks of networking: a lot of people aren't very good at it, so they ruin it for everyone else, and it is *exceptionally* time consuming. So, you must have a plan for your networking, and you must set priorities for whom you are willing to contact. Let's face it: you are a seasoned and valuable person, you can't just waste your time meeting with just anyone!

Many authors and advisors recommend relying almost exclusively on networking. Matthew "Matt" Bud, chairman of the Financial Executives Networking Group ("FENG") is probably the U.S', if not the world's, leading authority on networking. I would not go as far as to say that Matt recommends networking exclusively, but his view is the best odds for an out-of-work executive to find a new position is through networking. As previously mentioned earlier in this book, I don't go quite as far as Matt for two key reasons. First, if you live in a large city, getting to a networking meeting, finding a place to park, finding the office, actually having the meeting, retrieving your car and returning to your home or office can easily blow three or four hours. I've had many situations where two networking meetings consumed an entire day. This defeats our overarching strategy of getting large numbers working for us-we need to make far more than two contacts a day. Second, there will be days with no meetings and days with big gaps between meetings. This can become singularly depressing: *am I such a loser that I can't even get anyone to meet with me?* Having said that, Mr. Budd is correct, a great many more senior managers are likely to find a new position through networking than any other method. Further, it doesn't just work for executives. It also works for coders, sales associates, accountants, buyers and purchasing agents, chefs, funeral directors and attorneys. Just about everyone

In Chapter 4 you identified your contact list, and updated it with current information. Now it is time to press that list into service. Go through your list and mark the individuals most likely to know of opportunities. These might be association heads, lawyers, company presidents, human resource department staff, bankers–both traditional and investment–CPA firm partners, investors, venture capitalists, real estate agents (they are handling a home sale or family relocation) and local association chapter presidents. *Don't just include people you know. Include those people you don't know, identified in your research that you need to meet.*

<u>Getting the meetings</u>

Once you've developed your priority-ranked list, practice your script a few times, begin dialing, keeping the script where you can see it as your security blanket. Keep your eyes on the prize: you want to convince the person you are calling to carve out twenty minutes of time to meet so that you can learn about opportunities in your target industry and community. Further, you need to get the name of other potential key contacts. Most importantly, you want the individual who granted you time for the meeting to feel rewarded that you met and that you are a good candidate for someone.

<u>The Iron Law of Networking</u>

The Iron Law of Networking dictates that you do not go into a network meeting to ask for a job. *Do Not Violate This Law.* Why? The purpose of the meeting is to learn of opportunities, and obtain referrals to other individuals. Here is an example of a good networking meeting discussion between Ann, who is looking for a new position and Frank who is an executive who has agreed to meet her:

Ann: "Hi Frank, thank you so much for creating some time on your busy schedule for me, I really appreciate it. As you know, I'm looking for a new opportunity to apply my marketing skills and experience, ideally with a consumer packaged goods company, but my background is broad enough that I could handle a senior marketing role in some related industries. Your operation is certainly doing some very interesting things in that regard. I saw your new advertising and promotion program–and I'd like to know more about the industry trends as you see them. You must have increased your budget or achieved additional reach in some very creative way. I can give you my observations about what other companies are doing."

(Ann stops and waits for a response).

What makes this a good start to a network meeting?

- Ann gave sincere thanks for Frank taking the time to meet.
- Our candidate DID NOT ask for a job, or about job openings.
- Ann buttered up Frank a little by mentioning higher spending or increased reach in a creative way.
- Frank knows that Ann prepared for the meeting.
- Our candidate has something to trade: information about what Frank's competitors are doing.

- Now Frank is interested in the conversation because there is something in it for him.

The good networking conversation continues: Frank: "Well, Ann, first we've seen, as I'm sure you're aware, the entry of foreign competition from both Europe and Asia, with good products backed by strong balance sheets. So we've had to respond to that. We've made a concerted effort to reduce product defects and shorten development time for new products. A newer product line with fewer defects gave us marketing folks some new ammunition, we've been screaming about these issues to operations for years, but we couldn't get manufacturing and production to move fast enough. But when the Chinese started entering the market, you better believe it got the CEO's attention. Now we are making some progress and he held off the bean counters this year on our ad budget."

(Wow! Notice how much Ann has just learned! In any case, she has a basis for future conversations with others in the industry)

Ann: "You know Frank, we saw some of that, but probably not as directly as you, when that German company-you know those guys?- launched their high-end product. I'll tell you what was very successful for us. We scrapped our old display booth for the big trade shows and built a bigger, state of the art booth, got bigger space at the Dallas show and the Miami show, and brought everyone from the CEO on down to the shows for the entire length of the event. We got the best hotel suites and wined and dined our customers non-stop. Sure it was expensive, but we figured that the CEO from Frankfurt wasn't going to make both shows for the entire time, and even if their product line-up was a little stronger, we could out-sell and out-hustle them for one year while the product guys caught us up."

(Frank is very interested in this idea: he knows his trade show booth is now long in the tooth. He can "borrow" this idea for his company and look like a genius.)

Frank: "How did that go?" Ann: "It could not have gone better. The Germans' sent all their technical guys to man the booth, and their US sales team, but nobody else from Germany! Not a single senior person. The customers were impressed that our CEO was there talking to them. We stole a year from them. And they still don't know why they didn't have a better show".

After a few minutes of small talk, Ann can now ask for help, and be confident she will get it.

Ann: "Frank, this has been a great conversation. Who else do you think I should talk to? I'd like to stay in this industry, but, as I mentioned, if there is another that is closely aligned, I'd consider it."

At this point, Frank will certainly have some names. He may even volunteer to contact them for Ann!

At this point it is time to close. Three things must be done: first, leave a résumé and a business card: "I'd just like to drop this off in case you think of someone", second, get his business card, and third, thank him again for his time.

Ann: "May I have your business card? And I must thank you again for being so generous with your time."

Getting each business card is critical. It provides an email address and almost always direct dial phone number. Both are invaluable as you follow-up and fire-up exponential growth.

Now, that you've seen a model of a productive networking meeting, practice with someone you know, but in a real situation. Before you start cold calling strangers, schedule network meetings with people you know.

<u>The power of referral</u>

Getting in to see senior executives is exceptionally difficult. Referrals are a huge advantage in this effort. In many instances, a referral is the only chance one has of meeting an executive. Which of these sounds more promising?

Networker: "Hi, my name is Scott Kreger, and I'm calling for Mr. Smith."

Admin: "May I tell Mr. Smith what this is in reference to?"

Networker: "I'm an experienced marketing executive, and I would like to meet Mr. Smith to explore opportunities".

Or

Networker: "Hi, my name is Scott Kreger, and I'm calling for Mr. Smith."

Admin: "May I tell Mr. Smith what this is in reference to?"

Networker: "Mr. Jones, the President of your ad agency, Jones and Jones, recommended I give Mr. Smith a call immediately."

Which of those do you think has the better chance of success?

This is why networking is powerful. In your last job, which call would you have been more likely to take, the call from a stranger, or the call from a stranger who is using the name of someone who is on your Board of Directors?

Co-opt the gatekeeper into becoming your friend

If you are trying to see a senior executive, partner or company president, you have a tremendously skilled adversary: the administrative assistant. If you don't get this person on your side, you have no chance. You *must* win this person over.

When calling to set-up a network appointment, always get the admin's name, and correct spelling. Do not refer to him by his first name until he asks you to. If you can't get past the admin to have a phone call directly with your target, send your résumé and cover letter to the admin, not the target, with a note addressed to the admin asking for help in getting your résumé to the target manager. This changes your relationship vis-à-vis the admin: you have explicitly acknowledged his authority. My personal experience is that more of my résumés made it to the CEO via the admin than made it past an admin.

Following up to a networking meeting

The first, and most important follow-up is writing a thank you note to the person you met with. Not only is this common courtesy, it is a critical reinforcement of your marketing message. Hal Hassell, Chief Marketing Officer of IRON Solutions and an expert on networking, teaches that the rule your mother taught you about thank you notes is not appropriate for networking. Mom taught (that is, if your mom had really good manners) that you don't get to play with the new toy until you've written the thank you note. Hal recommends targeting a thank you note to arrive exactly one week after your meeting. Why one week later? That's when a good memory prompt might be most effective. The networking rule is then, that executives are exceptionally busy, and commitments they made to you for a lead or referral might get forgotten in the pressures of their day to day jobs. Therefore, a thank you note, mailed to arrive a week after the meeting, accomplishes multiple objectives.

My corollary to Hal Hassell's recommendation is that the note should be hand written. Never, NEVER, an email. You can find nice blank thank you cards at all card stores. Pick out a style that is businesslike. If your script-like mine-is illegible, then print. If you must, a typed letter on nice stationery is acceptable.

The message should be in the classic style of three short paragraphs. The opening should thank the executive for taking time to meet. The middle should be a statement of next steps ("I've already got a call into Mr. Smith") or ("Please let me know when you have had an opportunity to contact Mr. Smith on my behalf"). The final should be an additional thank you.

Insider tip: thank you notes should be about the recipient, not the sender. For example: "Thank you for taking the time to meet with me." Not "I want to thank you…". Make the note all about them. Their knowledge, their calendar, their generosity.

The second follow-up is to report back on actions. If Mr. Jones gave you a referral to Mr. Smith, after the meeting occurred you must let Mr. Jones know. Some experts on networking don't agree with me on this step. My rationale is that Mr. Jones has made two investments in you: first the time to meet with you and second an important referral. His reputation with Mr. Smith will be affected by your behavior. So, a brief email to Mr. Jones is in order. It should:

- State that you did indeed follow-up and meet with Mr. Smith.
- State that it was a good and productive meeting.
- Ask that he please let you know of anyone else you should meet.

This demonstrates that you took action and therefore were worthy of his time investment. Further, if you provided something of value to Mr. Smith in that meeting, you have furthered Mr. Jones reputation, making him even more of a supporter in the future!

<u>Directed Networking</u>

An interesting subset of our topic is Directed Networking ("DN"). In DN, one has learned of a specific position of interest (or even a rumor of a specific position of interest). In these cases, the cold call scripts must change to a different request for action, and research priorities modified to reflect a changed priority. (See Chapter 19 for tips on researching businesses.) In the course of looking for a new position, more than likely you will only learn of 5-6 positions of great interest in the course of a year (!)[3] When one of these opportunities reveals itself, you must change the time allocation on your weekly calendar immediately.

On DN calls to network contacts, you must inform your contact that you have learned of a specific position at Company Z, and are looking for an introduction at a senior level at that firm. These calls tend to be highly productive. If indeed the contact knows someone in that firm, they usually make the contact. Or, they refer you to someone else who they believe is likely to be able to help you. In either case, you are a sure winner: you've established additional contacts. Of course, all the rules we've previously covered about the use of time and appropriate follow-up to these contacts apply.

I've found DN calls and emails to search firms to be almost as effective! Large search firms hate to learn there was a search they didn't even get a shot at, and all firms hate it if an existing client uses a competitive firm for a search. And, they are all desperate for business in this environment, all of which works in your favor for a DN call.

When I was previously out of work, I heard a rumor that a very large and very successful Big Chain Retailer was looking for a new executive in my field. I considered their headquarters location to be a very attractive place to live, and had no question that the compensation package would be very attractive. I sprang into action, changing everything conceivable in my schedule. I sent a customized résumé via overnight delivery to the CEO's assistant. I placed calls to friends, contacts, and associates asking for connections into the company– or for a networking contact to the company.

After that was underway, I began contacting search firms that I knew specialized in retailing. If I had the opportunity to speak to a search consultant who I have known over the years, I stated directly that I had learned that Big Chain Retailer was looking for a new senior executive, and, that if they had the search, I'd like to be considered for the opportunity. If I only made it to voice mail, I left a similar message, but without giving out the name [Big Chain Retailer] of the hiring company, so that they would have to call me back to learn more.

Given the number of search firms out there, the odds of course that any single firm had that assignment were quite low. However, the competitive nature of search consultants is such that most all of them either took the call or called back. So, at a minimum I established an updated contact, keeping recency high. Occasionally, I learned of another opportunity at a competitive search firm (meaning that the person I was talking to had lost that search to a competitor) that I could look into. While I did not get that position at Big Chain Retailer, I did make a number of valuable impressions.

You now have all the tools required to begin networking. You've polished your résumé, reviewed key performance statistics, practiced answers to typical interview questions, prepared your interview wardrobe and gotten into shape. Start dialing!

Chapter 15 Direct Mail

In Chapter 5 you developed your contact list. Now is the time to really put that list to work generating job leads and opportunities.

Let me be clear: if you don't make 2,000 or more contacts through email, direct mail, website hits, networking groups or networking meetings, you are a sissy and not serious about finding a new position. (I'm assuming that you are prepared to run a national campaign. If you are committed to remaining where you are, you won't push that many contacts. At the risk of sounding harsh, as a result you may be out of work for a very long time.)

Tactic one: the cover letter (or cover email)

The audience you are trying to reach receives hundreds, or perhaps thousands of résumés or applications a year. When you were between searches, did you ever advertise for a position and receive thousands of résumés? What happened? *You looked for reasons to screen out candidates, not to include them.* That screening process is about to happen to you! How do you fight back? By having a powerful cover letter (or cover email) that summarizes the value you would bring to the company in a very concise and focused way. That cuts through the clutter of hundreds-or thousands-of résumés from competitors for the job. As we covered before in Chapter 6, I believe in maintaining and using multiple résumés. (Most job websites allow one to publish multiple résumés and submit different ones depending on the job posting.)

My recommendation is that you do both: prepare highly-customized cover letters for each situation, and customize a résumé when: you become aware of a particular position of interest, and you have enough specific knowledge of position requirements to permit you to tailor your résumé and select the accomplishments that put you in the best possible light.

I obtained a position as CFO of a public company in what I consider to be a most unlikely way: I responded to an ad in the <u>Wall Street Journal</u>! I placed the exclamation point at the end of the last sentence because, in over 30 years of work and far too many job changes, I had never had any positive results responding to an advertisement. I'm not even completely sure why I responded to that one other than it caught my eye and I considered myself an excellent candidate given the requirements specified in the ad. The ad directed responses to an email address. So I carefully summarized my experience and accomplishments that were directly related to the position specifications shown in the ad and emailed it away. Much to my surprise I heard from the company within hours, had phone interviews later on that day and more phone interviews that week; visited the company the following week, met with board members the week after that, and started work within thirty days of the initial contact!

While I've never been told, I credit my cover letter for getting me to the top of the stack. The following exhibits are designed to aid you in developing your own cover letters. Exhibits 15-1-3 present samples.

Exhibit 15-1 Blind Mailing to a Company

Mr. Marion Hale
Chief Executive Officer
Global Service Corp
200 Park Ave
NY NY 10001

Mr. Hale:

Could Global services use a proven sales and marketing executive with hands-on international expertise?

I'm an experienced marketing and sales executive with over 25 years of successfully planning and executing marketing programs that grow revenue and profits and capture market share.

In my most recent position as EVP – Marketing at Big Diamonds, the marketing programs developed in my group drove a compound 18% revenue gain over three years, increasing sales by a total of $32 million, while reducing advertising and promotional expense from 6.5% of revenue to 4%.

I also have extensive international experience, having held a broad range of marketing positions including positions responsible for entering international markets and growing revenue in Asia and Europe. In my most recent prior marketing position as SVP Marketing for a multinational supply chain company, we successfully entered Japan, Korea, Hong Kong and mainland China in twenty-four months, achieved breakeven in each country within twelve months and profit within twenty-four months, and established our brand in each locale.

While you may not current opening, you know the value that the right team members can add. May I meet with you so that you become acquainted with my background in case a future need arises?

I've attached a résumé for your consideration, or you can get a quick feel for my qualifications at my website: www.scottkreger.com. Please feel free to call me anytime on my mobile phone at (123) 123-1234.
Sincerely,
Scott Kreger

Exhibit 12-2 Broadcast mailing to search firms

Mr. Hunter
Managing Director
Hunter Partners
200 Park Ave.
New York NY 10002

Mr. Hunter:

I'm an experienced marketing and sales executive with over 25 years of successfully planning and executing marketing programs that grow revenue and profits and capture market share.

In my most recent position as EVP–Marketing at Big Diamonds, the marketing programs developed in my group drove a compound 18% revenue gain over three years, increasing sales by a total of $32 million, while reducing advertising and promotional expense from 6.5% of revenue to 4%.

I also have extensive international experience having held a broad range of marketing positions, including positions responsible for entering and growing revenue in Asia and Europe.

In my most recent prior marketing position as SVP Marketing for a multinational supply chain company, we successfully entered Japan, Korea, Hong Kong and mainland China in twenty-four months, achieved breakeven in each country within twelve months and profit within twenty-four months, and established our brand in each locale.

My most recent compensation was a base of $300,000, a bonus opportunity of 50% of base, and a substantial stock option position, but I'm willing to be flexible for the right growth opportunity. My wife and I would consider an international posting with a company committed to international growth.

Can I come by and catch you up in person? I'd like your advice on who I should meet, and what companies you see doing interesting things.

I've attached a résumé for your review, or you can get a quick feel for my qualifications at my website: www.scottkreger.com. Please feel free to call me anytime on my mobile phone at (123) 123-1234.

Thank you for your consideration.

Sincerely,

Scott Kreger

Exhibit 15-3 Mailing to a Known Contact

Mr. Ed Rose
Chief Executive Officer
Serality
225 Winter Street
Hopkinton MA 01748
Ed:

I'm dropping you a note to let you know that I'm a free agent again, and looking for an opportunity to put my 25+ years of marketing experience to work.

As you know, I've held a broad range of marketing positions, including entering and growing revenue in Asia and Europe.

In my most recent position as EVP–Marketing at BigDiamonds, the marketing programs developed in my group drove a compound 18% revenue gain over three years, increasing sales by a total of $32 million, while reducing advertising and promotional expense from 6.5% of revenue to 4%.

In my most recent prior marketing position as SVP Marketing for a multinational supply chain company, we successfully entered Japan, Korea, Hong Kong and mainland China in twenty-four months, achieved breakeven in each country within twelve months and profit within twenty-four months, and established our brand in each locale.

Since we last worked together, my compensation has increased some: at BigDiamonds my compensation package included a base of $300,000, a bonus opportunity of 50% of base, and a substantial stock option position. But as always I'm willing to be flexible for the right growth opportunity.

Can I come by and catch you up in person? I'd like your advice on who I should meet, and what companies you see doing interesting things.

I'll give you a call on Thursday the 1st. If you need to reach me, call me anytime on my mobile phone at (123) 123-234.

Thanks!

Best regards,

Scott Kreger

A few things to note from these letters. First, the accomplishments from the work you did in Chapter 5 become a core component of the letters. Second, the tone changes slightly for each, from very formal in the company mailing to the more familiar in a mailing to a known contact. And third, we reuse elements from one to the next.

It is this ability to use your PC and word processing software to quickly modify cover letters to tailor them to the audience that makes them so easy to prepare. And, since many applicants don't spend adequate time on cover letters, this is a chance to stand out.

Suppose that one of your networking contacts has informed you that Blevins Global Trading is looking for a senior sales executive to lead its European selling efforts. The position requires an executive that has solid international experience, knowledge of technology markets and buyers and a reputation as a team builder. You review your accomplishments from Chapter 5, copy a couple into your *Blind Mailing to a Company* letter, and viola – you have Exhibit 15-4.

Exhibit 15-4 Mailing for a Specific Opportunity

Mr. G.W. Blevins
Chief Executive Officer
Blevins Global Trading
1800 Chreval
Germantown TN 37101

Mr. Blevins:

My background and skills are an excellent match to the requirements for your opening for a SVP–European Sales.

I have extensive international experience having held a broad range of sales and marketing positions, including positions responsible for entering international markets and growing revenue in Asia and Europe. I have lived and worked in both and Europe and Asia, where I built strong, local management teams in technology and consumer goods businesses.

In my most recent position as EVP–Marketing at Big Diamonds, the marketing programs developed in my group drove a compound 18% revenue gain over three years, increasing sales by a total of $32 million, while reducing advertising and promotional expense from 6.5% of revenue to 4%.

In my most recent prior marketing position as SVP Sales and Marketing for a multinational supply chain company, we successfully entered Japan, Korea, Hong Kong and mainland China in twenty-four months, achieved breakeven in each country within twelve months and profit within twenty-four months, and established our brand in each locale.

My wife and I would consider an international posting with a company committed to international growth.

I've attached a résumé for your consideration, or you can get a quick feel for my qualifications at my website: www.scottkreger.com. Please feel free to call me anytime on my mobile phone at (123) 123-1234.

Sincerely,

Best regards,

Scott Kreger

Each of these letters carefully recognizes the needs of the audience in both content and tone.

For the company, we have carefully selected accomplishments that we believe to be most relevant, and our tone is businesslike and direct.

For search firms the tone is serious; we address issues like relocation directly and disclose compensation. And we describe the breadth of our background to expand the universe of positions we will be considered for. (Search firms are the worst at pigeon-holing candidates; you must constantly guard against only being considered for the same job you previously occupied in the same industry.)

For known contacts we can be more relaxed and confident. Since we talk to some contacts more frequently than others, we need to include some key points to stimulate their memory about recent positions and desired opportunities.

<u>Email covers</u>

This tactic works equally well, but slightly differently, when communicating by email. The key differences are that:

- Emails must be shorter
- One must decide whether or not to include attachments
- Formatting needs to be simpler
- Electronic signatures are appropriate

As discussed in Chapter 6, if you have great experience, I do not believe that a résumé has to be compacted into two, much less one page. However, email is to be used for brief, concise messages. Your targeted recipient could be receiving the message in a variety of ways ranging from a desktop with a fast connection, to a hotel room thousands of miles away with a slow connection, to an IPad, smartphone, or any of a variety of other devices. Those mobile devices do not lend themselves to reading long copy, and some can't access attachments easily. Respect both your reader and the unwritten rule of the media–make email messages very taut.

In many cases, it is better to simply cut and paste your résumé into the body of the email. There are strong opinions both ways on this matter. With viruses lurking in attachments, recipients are increasingly reluctant to click on an attached document. But long emails tend to be annoying as well. Whenever possible, determine the user's preference and go with it.

Not all email programs support all fonts and symbols. If you chose to paste your résumé into the body of the email, chose a common font, like Arial or Times New Roman, replace any unusual characters you are using for bullet points, and eliminate any formats other than straight text. That is, if for example, your résumé is set up as a table with columns for dates of employment and another column for accomplishments, you must convert that to an old-fashioned straight-text format. This way, you may be confident that the recipient won't receive an unformatted string of gobbledy-gook. An excellent alternative if you have the capability is to convert your document to a PDF file. Those do an outstanding job of preserving formatting across a variety of devices.

Or, if you now have an on-line résumé on your own website, then create a good email, forget the résumé and send a link!

<u>Use the Technology</u>

I don't know why, but it seems that my email software frequently turns the spell check feature off. No problem if I'm sending an email to my sister, but a disaster if I'm communicating about a job opportunity. I don't know about you, but I assume the worst of any candidate who has a spelling error on his cover letter or cover email. Make absolutely positive that every document you send has been spell-checked.[4]

If you are using Microsoft Outlook as your email tool, use the signature feature to create and insert a complete signature or a "V-Card". Complete means that you can be contacted in any way: phone, email or USPS. When you create and enable an auto-signature, your contact info will be inserted at the end of all your emails. Nothing could be worse than to find a position that you are a great candidate for, develop a customized letter to the employer, fire it off, the employer reads your message and is motivated to action, and then not be able to find your phone number or email address instantly.

In my version of Outlook, automatic signatures are set up under the "Tools" menu. Click on Tools, then select "Options". Under Options, select the "Mail Format" tab. On that page you will find the "Signature" section. Click on "New", then "Create New Signature" then "Next". Fill in the form with your name as you would in a formal memorandum, then mailing address, phone number and finally your email address. If you have a website, then include that too. Click "Apply". From then on, your email address should appear automatically at the bottom of your emails. Many folks now add a link to their LinkedIn account, and Skype contact information. Those are good additions.

In the same menu are directions for creating a "v card", which readers can simply click and add to their contact file. That is an excellent alternative to the signature format.

Insider tip 1: Create a tagline. Professional sales executives and marketing professionals know the power of metaphors and taglines. Spend a few minutes to think about your value to an enterprise: what are you really, really good at that someone will pay for. Remember the famous marketing story about Canon. Canon created the EOS Rebel series of cameras that were simpler to use compared to the increasingly feature and complexity rich cameras available at the time. Why? Because consumers don't want great cameras–consumers want great pictures. Employers don't want more payroll; they want someone to get some work done that currently isn't being done, or done well. If you can summarize your value in a short phrase–then include it in your digital signature at the end. Example – for a tax professional, "Helping companies cut their tax bills". What business doesn't want to pay less tax? Or, for a six sigma quality black belt: "Raising the bar on product quality"?

From our man Scott Kreger:

Scott Kreger
Cell: (123) 123-1234
Scott@scottkreger.com
Helping business grow international sales

Test, Test,Test

Send emails, cover letters and résumés to yourself and to trusted friends. Carefully check the formatting spelling and contents. Remember, even the best spell-checker software won't spot the wrong word if it is spelled correctly. Check your headers and footers. I discovered, after sending a few hundred letters and résumés, that I had misspelled my own street name in the address line of my résumé!

Once you have mailed to your trusted contacts, follow-up on anything they have noticed in formatting and spelling as well as content. After all the errors have been corrected and double-checked, ask those advisors for a no-hold barred critique. What is too flowery, too long, not hard-hitting, or not convincing in your message? For that matter-is the message clear? Thoughtfully examine their input and recommendations. Remove your ego from your writing.[5]

Naming Your Attachment

If you are emailing a cover letter and attaching a résumé, give it a smart name. It simply isn't a good idea to have something like "résumé.doc" as an attachment. Use your name-scottkreger.doc–so that an interviewer receiving thousands of résumés can go back and find yours in their electronic in-basket.

Responding to an Internet Posting

During your nightly and weekly trolling through Internet job sites, it is likely there will be a position of interest at least weekly, if not daily. Those responses require an extra step. Assume that some of the most attractive positions will interest *thousands* of candidates!

Insider tip 2: A reminder about keywords: internet job postings frequently use keyword electronic search to identify candidates to screen further. If your cover letter and résumé don't contain those keywords, you won't even get to digital first base. Review the wording of the posting carefully, looking for the nouns and adjectives that indicate the employer's areas of interest. Does the posting say "proven project manager skills"? Experienced Java programmer? Fluent in Mandarin? Seek out the 10-15 words that tell you the critical skills they are looking for. Those exact phrases must appear in both your résumé and your email cover letter.

<u>Standing Out</u>

Again, there may be thousands of applications for the position you want. In addition to carefully tailoring your resume and cover, there are other tricks you might employ. Graphic artists, website designers and fashion merchants frequently design envelops to stand out. Or include links to websites presenting their designs and portfolios. A simple technique is to add a thoughtful subject line in the email. Instead of just writing "Re: job posting 106" perhaps "Proven Account Manager for Posting 106". Consider getting creative in the subject line, just not too cute.

As a matter of routine, most of my business correspondence is sent in 8.5 by 11 colored envelopes, with commemorative stamps. Does anyone actually notice? I'm not sure, but it doesn't cost much more and I don't plan to stop.

Think of ways that your response might be more likely to be found in a crowded email inbox or USPS in basket.

<u>The Blistering Direct Mail Marketing Campaign</u>

All word processing software has some kind of "mail merge" feature that allows one to create a mailing list and send the same letter to multiple parties, but individually customized by name and address. In Microsoft Word 2010 this can be done with the "Mail Merge Wizard" in the mail merge section. (The Mail Merge feature is a significant improvement over previous versions of Windows and Word, in which Mail Merge was harder than calculus; however, it is still rather difficult to use, so plan on spending some time getting control of this, and be prepared for a fair amount of frustration.)

Step 1 Go to the "Mailings" drop down menu and click on "Start Mail Merge". Then click on "Letters". Click "Select Contacts".

Step 2 It should now show a box "Mail Merge Recipients". This list can be sorted and filtered by any of the fields. Sort as needed.[8]

Step 3 Review the names that appear in the drop down window. When I do this on my system, the list is, well, screwy. I have no idea what order the list is in… If your experience is like mine, it may take some work to clean it up.

I recommend that you only select two or three names to test merging and printing with so that you don't waste time, money and paper on the next few steps. Add an "Address Block" and a "Greeting Block". (Here is another place I had some weirdness: I had to advance to the feature where you "preview" your letter and then return to this screen for the addressing and greeting function to kick in–but it eventually did.) Alternatively, Mail Merge gives you the opportunity to input a list by clicking the "Type a new list" button.

Step 4 The next screen will ask that you edit recipients. This must be done one item at a time.

Step 5 Click on "Address Block" to format addresses.

Step 6 The "Address Block" gives you several options for Mr. and Ms., first name or entire name, etc. I found that no formula really worked well as I moved through my contacts which included individuals I know well and some that are business contacts I don't know as well.. Fortunately, Mail Merge gives you an option to edit items to achieve an individualized look while still using computer power to streamline the job. Nonetheless, count on several hours to do a sizable mailing.

Step 7 Print and start folding and stamping! (Remember that there is also a feature in the Tools menu on the same line as Mail Merge, e.g. "Letters and Mailing" that assists in preparing envelopes, which you'll want to do at the same time that you are printing letters.)

A final point: There are still a lot of writing purists in the business world. Bad grammar, misspelling, run-on sentences–any and all of these will look sloppy to the discerning reader. Those who think like that (you can include me in that group) will have a concern as to whether the candidate making those language and grammatical mistakes has appropriate attention to detail or thoroughness. It might be sufficient to eliminate one as a candidate. Be sure to check your cover letters and cover emails thoroughly before sending.

Now let's go to the hardest part of searching for a new position.

Chapter 16 Cold Calls

"...but I would attack them, for I hold it an established maxim that there is three to one in favour of the party attacking". Alexander Hamilton

In Chapter 5 you prepared your "Touch Base" phone script. In this chapter, we'll wrap up the remaining script and began our aggressive phone call campaign.

The Cold Call script is the most difficult. If you worked in a call center at some point in your life, then cold calling might not be intimidating. For almost everyone else, including experienced sales executives; cold calling is brutally hard work. Why? Because you will suffer an astonishing level of rejection. It is for this reason that I've saved the cold call for last. After you've built some confidence presenting yourself in your "touch base" calls and your networking calls, you are better prepared to move to the big leagues of cold calling.

Your objectives in cold calling are to get appointments to learn more about the business, and ultimately to identity opportunities either within the firm or a referral to someone in another firm.

First though, our script must give the recipient some powerful reasons to take the call. That means some research on the company. (Refer to Chapter 19 to learn how to do in-depth research on a company).

My friend Rob Williford likes to use topical articles to base his cold call scripts. He has his target list of companies and when he sees an article in the local paper or business press, it gives him a reason to make a contact. Combined with his previous research, he is prepared for both the call and the possibility of an immediate meeting.[9][10]

Cold caller: "Hi, this is Scott Kruger, and I'm calling for Ms. Williams."

Admin: "May I tell Ms. Williams what this is in reference to?"

Cold caller: "I've been following and researching your company and its competitors for some time now, and saw the article in yesterday's Wall Street

<u>Journal</u> which confirms my conclusions about the direction of the industry. I'd like to speak to Ms. Williams about industry direction."

While companies and individuals respond to cold calling in different ways, a good generality is that the higher your target individual is in the company, the harder she will be to reach. In fact, I have had some occasions trying to reach a company President where the switchboard not only wouldn't connect me to the President or his assistant; they wouldn't disclose the assistant's name! (My direct, personal experience is that these are excellent opportunities for stock short-selling. If I had immediately shorted the stock of companies behaving this way, I would have profited immensely, and with no exceptions!)[11]

Given the degree of difficulty of reaching the desired contact, the more critical it is that the script be smart, courteous, brief and compelling.

Insider tip one: My personal experience is, and my informal polls report that well over half of voice calls go to voice mail. Develop and practice a voice mail script along with your live script. Example: "Hi, this is Scott Kreger. It's Wednesday, July 23rd, I'm sorry I missed you. I've been following and researching your company and its competitors for some time now, and saw the article in yesterday's <u>Wall Street Journal</u> which confirms my conclusions about the direction of the industry. I am looking for a new position which will utilize my extensive direct marketing experience, and I believe my background is a great match with the strategy you are implementing. Can we meet? Call me anytime at 123-1234. I'll also try reaching you again. Again, it's Scott Kruger 123-1234."

Insider tip two: call early and late–particularly to reach senior executives. Most senior executives work longer hours than their assistants do and frequently answer their own phones before and after hours. One controller of a global company I know is generally in his office by six am. Managers of the global subsidiaries know that he can be reached then, and call him long before U.S. business hours. If you are having trouble reaching a critical executive, try his number early, late and on Saturday.

Insider tip three: many phone mail systems can be gamed to reveal direct dial numbers. Hacking the CEO's phone number is a game best played after eight PM or so. If you get the magic alphabetic directory, you are half way there. Frequently, upon spelling the name of your target, the phone system will state the extension. If that fails, try all the combinations of pressing 1, 2 etc. just to see what happens. About one in five times it is something good.

Insider tip four: intentionally get to the wrong extension, act surprised and ask to be transferred to the right place. Recently, I tried to get to the CEO of a national restaurant chain. The phone system was a horror show of "dial one for customer complaints; dial two for advertising; three for payroll," etc. None sounded like a formula to reach the CEO, and none offered a way to reach an operator. So, I dialed the marketing department, and, when reaching a pleasant human, stated "Oh, I've dialed the wrong extension. I was trying to reach Mr. Smith's office". They connected me immediately.

Insider tip five: many executives check their own voice mail rather than have an admin check it. Further, increasingly enterprises don't hire admins but rather expect the executive to perform that function herself. Either way, by calling late in the evening or early in the morning, you increase the odds that the executive will personally retrieve and listen to your message.

In Chapter 7 we covered scheduling calls in the morning and afternoon, to maximize availability of targets on the east and west coast. As your search gathers momentum and your network size expands, we should modify priorities. Logically, they should be:

- Referrals from networking meetings.
- Executives you know who can help you find another position.
- Someone you have an introduction to in a target company. (This, in turn, should be ranked by the companies you are most interested in.)
- Someone who can help you get to talk to a target company.
- Search firm executives you know well who will help you.
- Cold calls on companies.
- Networking calls where you have some connections
- Cold networking calls.
- Calls to search firms following up on résumé mailings.

My recommendations are different from a lot of other texts and coaches, so let me explain. If you decide that you disagree, that is fine, just make sure of two things: the priority you set is logical, not emotional, and doesn't reflect distaste for networking, or cold calling; and second, that you adhere to the priorities once you set them.

1. Networking referrals. I have this first for a simple reason: you owe the person who gave you the referral a prompt follow-up. He is personally invested in you and you must respect that investment

2. Executives who can help. This really is self-evident. Meeting with executives with whom you have a relationship and who are willing to help is the fastest path to a new position. (Unfortunately, even the best of us generally don't have very many of those contacts.)

3. An existing personal contact in a target company. Once you've developed your target list of companies, and researched the list, this is a critical priority. An insider can flesh out the critical politics, identify the real decision-makers, and the individuals whose performance gives them more influence than their title might otherwise suggest. Combine this with the results of the research you've performed and you have surprising insight into the company.

4. A new networking contact within a targeted company. More often than the first three, you've identified a company that you are interested in, but don't have a good contact. Someone who can open the door for you will be far more efficient than cold calling.

5. Known search firm contacts. Despite the state of the search business at this writing, the most senior positions still generally are handled by search executives. They, of course, only have time to sell, so they budget their time carefully, and don't eagerly look for out-of-work folks to talk to. If you have one of these precious contacts, by all means, use it. Be sure to be completely prepared and use your contact's time very wisely. (Search firms have their own lexicon for those who are out-of-work and looking for a new position. Frequently, those are known as "on the beach".)

6. Cold calling firms. This is the grunt work of job hunting. I have it a lower priority for two reasons, first, it consumes a shocking amount of time, since you will be turned down, screened-out by admins and shunted to voice mail so often, and second, since the success ratio is

so small, and the ego damage is so extensive for so many people, that you must schedule this activity in a way to not harm your overall effort. Nonetheless, even with a low batting average, this method still yields a lot of jobs for the persistent caller who can withstand the ego assault. Since this method does produce real results, it makes number six on our list.

7. Networking calls. This reconnoitering activity is extensively covered in Chapter 14. By definition, these are previously identified contacts; your success rate in making contact then should be far higher. And, since networking meetings are very time-consuming, you can only schedule a limited number per week.

8. Cold networking call. The odds of setting up networking meetings with total strangers are low. Due to the likelihood isn't good, use this as calendar filler.

9. Cold calls on search firms. If it is hard to talk to a search firm person you know, you can only imagine the degree of difficulty of reaching one that you don't. Only after you've done everything else, tackle this one.

More than likely you will need multiple cold call scripts. There are two themes for you to develop: 1) a reason for the gatekeeper to let you talk to your target, and 2) something of value to exchange with your target. Did your company research point out something interesting? Do you have some industry scuttlebutt worth sharing? Do you know of highly regarded individuals on the move within the industry? Have you learned of new product introductions that your target company might not have heard of yet?

I'm a voracious reader. I'm on the email distribution list for several brokerage firms that cover the industry I'm currently in. I read all their reports even though I generally have to do that at night or on weekends. But, they keep me up to date on competitor performance, trends and executive turnover. There are about twenty brokerage houses that cover various public companies that we compete with. To my surprise, when I joined this firm, only the reports of a couple of Wall Street firms were being widely disseminated and read. So, it was easy to learn quickly some info that many of my peers didn't even know.

You may find that your research, even though it only accesses public data, still turns up information that your target contact hasn't learned. After all, he may be working 80 hours a week trying to keep his job! You have the time to do the industry research, scan the industry periodicals that are piling up on his desk, check the postings on stock message boards, visit competitor websites, and otherwise gather breaking news and intriguing information he hasn't seen yet. Tossing in a teaser data point might just help get you a networking meeting. Therefore, when leaving that voice mail on your target's voice mail system, mentioning that "I saw that an old friend of mine who is an expert in ecommerce just joined one of your largest competitors, and I think I know where that is headed" might be just the kind of market intelligence that gets you into the door.

Cold calling businesses

If you've targeted a firm, but simply can't get a connection or referral to anyone in the company then, use a more direct approach. "Hi, this is ____ and I'm exploring new opportunities in the ____ industry. I'm meeting industry leaders to get their view on the direction of the business, so that I can target my job search wisely. May I have a half hour on your calendar to get your opinion on industry direction? Thanks!"

Obviously, you must demonstrate great flexibility and be willing to meet early, after work, or anytime in between.

Cold calling search firms

Simply don't bother cold calling search firms until you have mailed and emailed your résumé. Then, you can follow up with a call. "Hi, this is Scott Kreger, I forwarded my résumé to you last week, and I wanted to make a personal connection". Don't be disappointed if you never get through or a return call. Unless you are an absolute brand name executive–Bill Gates, Jack Welch, Indra Nooyi, Sergey Brin, Jamie Dimon, Melissa Mayer, Mark Zuckerberg-well, you get the picture-they aren't too likely to return your call unless they (a) have read your résumé, and (b) have a search that matches it.

If they do return your call, make sure you have your accomplishments handy, along with a crisp statement on the type of position you would be interested in. "I've spent several years in international consumer marketing, and have expat experience. I would be most valuable to a consumer-oriented business looking to enter or expand globally."

Conversations with retained search firms are very important, and covered initially in Chapter 12 and again in detail in Chapter 19.

<u>Cold networking calls</u>

The cold networking call is quite similar to cold calling on firms, except that you look for a likely hiring decision maker. So, if you are a programmer, call the Chief Information Officer. If you are an accountant, call the Controller or CFO.

This script may reflect a little more about you than the cold call on the firm's script. Our fearless cold caller Scott searches his target's SEC filings and company website, reviews LinkedIn, and finds an individual with the intriguing title of Group President-International. That sounds like someone who might hire a marketing executive with extensive international background. Scott then places his call at 7:45 a. m., hoping to reach the Group President before his gatekeeper administrative assistant arrives. The script Scott will use is "Good morning, I'm Scott Kreger, I have an extensive background in international marketing, and I'm looking for a new career opportunity. I've done research on your industry, and I'm meeting with international executives in the area to get their views on industry direction. May I have thirty minutes of your time?"

Again, Scott is direct and concise-two valuable traits time-pressed individuals are looking for.

<u>Practice</u>

If you have ever done cold-call selling, you know the importance of scripts and practice. Call centers use scientifically developed scripts to achieve the best response to their calls and emails. (Call center software enables real-time script result comparisons. That is, they start calling with three or four scripts and quickly abandon the scripts with the worst performance in favor of the highest performing script). Before you start dialing, practice. Practice in front of a mirror. Make sure that you smile as you practice, and when you make the actual calls. It sounds trite but it does come through in your voice. Standing while calling will also change the tenor, confidence and tone of your voice and message. Remember, you are a very valuable asset that someone seeks to acquire. Never sound apologetic, defensive or defeated.

<u>The Pep Talk</u>

Nothing is harder than cold-calling to find employment. Some successful executives make it a scoring exercise and create rewards for themselves. For example, successfully reaching a target is a homerun, and worth celebrating for a moment.

Then ten calls in the morning, ten in the afternoon with two actual live conversations equals a highly productive day. At that rate you are creating forty-plus individuals a month who know about you and will likely remember you if they learn of an opportunity.

As with all our contact methods, you will need a follow-up approach with your new contacts. A thank-you card for taking the time to take your call. (I might compromise here with some job seekers who argue that an mail is satisfactory in this situation.)

However, face-to-face meetings resulting from a cold call require the usual follow-up including a more formal thank-you note and periodic updates on your progress.

Let's have a refresher on your tech equipment needs.

Chapter 17 Equipment

"Success demands a high level of logistical and organizational competence." General George S. Patton, Jr.

We noted in Chapter 4 that you are now an Army of One, constantly networked. Let's talk about the equipment required.

First, a smartphone. I assume you have one and you know how to use it. It goes without saying that you must be able to use it to a real extent-you'll look really foolish if the interviewer starts asking about using Siri on your IPhone and you barely know how to make a phone call and have never sent a text. Your smartphone will be on close to, or all of, 24 hours a day. That way network partners, recruiters and employers can reach you at any time by voice, text, email or IM. Remember, in the new technological age as you build your enormous network, you must always be connected. Your phone goes where you go and is on all the time, except when you are in church or your children's graduation. And then you should consider leaving it on vibrate until you obtained and started your next position.

Second, your personal website or blog. I strongly recommend that you develop your own website. It took me a few days to do mine, but it helped me stand out from the competitors, positions me as technologically current, and allows more detail, use of color and graphics, links etc. that generate interest far beyond a simple résumés. Even if you don't build your own site, you should make every effort to control your name. If your name is John Smith, it is probably too late: but the permutations of initials, first and middle names, and dot-com, dot-net, dot-us and dot-biz mean that for each name combination you create, there are multiple registration opportunities. You should grab one of these ASAP before someone else does.

While there are a number of hosting services that make this process surprisingly easy, three are worth mentioning because of their low cost and their investment in templates that simplify the process of posting a pretty cool personal site with your résumé: Go Daddy (www.godaddy.com), 1and1.com (www.1and1.com) and Network Solutions (www.networksolutions.com). (Disclosure: I have no commercial interest and don't get a commission from these sites, although, if you work for Go Daddy, 1and1 or Network Solutions

I wouldn't mind if you want to add me to your payroll.) [12] There are numerous others and the competitive landscape in this arena changes rapidly, so do some homework. If you know WordPress or TypePad, there are even more options available to you.

Third, a separate telephone line. If you have outplacement, voice mail and phone lines are covered for you. Otherwise, get a clean phone line for exclusive use for finding a new position. Record an upbeat, voice mail greeting for those times you are not available for calls. One senior executive that I know well, who has been looking for work for an extended time, has a voice mail greeting that sounds like it was recorded immediately prior to going to a funeral home for the service of a late best friend. It badly needs to be replaced by something with more enthusiasm.

Fourth, a fast internet connection with email. This is a must, and frankly more important than the others. *Seventy-five percent of your communications on your next position will be conducted via email.* Probably ninety percent of your research on companies will be done on line. Result: faster the connection the better. Most areas of the world now offer high-speed connections to homes via DSL, cable or satellite. You are going to need all the bandwidth you can afford.

Insider tip: be smart in selection of your email address. I don't know what is in someone's mind when they send a job-related email from an address like "racoonboy@yahoo.com", or "hotbootie@gmail.com", but I don't think it is helpful in landing that next position.

Fifth, organizer software. Most of America is now standardized on Microsoft Outlook, although there are some excellent alternatives. Experienced sales folks may want to employ their favorite contact management tool. No matter which one you use, there are some critical actions you must take. First, as you get business cards from network contacts, recruiters, interviewers and so on, make sure to update your contacts file. Second, frequently back up that data, so that a hard drive failure or other technical challenge doesn't leave you suicidal over lost data. (*This cannot be over-emphasized! Recently, my trusty notebook computer failed. While it was in the repair shop, my trusty back-up desktop was infected by a virus, despite my having current anti-virus and a spyware product. Offline backup can be an antidote to suicide when your real-time systems fail.)* Third, all of the contact managers have a comments area. Use it to include memory prompts such as the date of last contact, admin's name, number and email address (particularly important) and follow-up dates.[13]

I still keep most of my most important notes, addresses and follow-ups in some kind of paper files or my Franklin Planner. But I update Microsoft Outlook regularly with key contact information. And I back that up regularly, both on the cloud and on a removable hard drive. There are so many cloud solutions to file backup that I won't list them. Use one.

Sixth, a laptop or tablet. You probably already have one. If not, I recognize that this can be a substantial investment, particularly if you are out of work and budget-constrained. And the technology obsolescence cost is painful. Therefore this may really only make sense for those readers who are conducting a national search and are traveling extensively for interviews. Or for those of you have landed consulting assignments to generate some cash. It is also useful in maintaining or improving your skills as you look for a permanent position. A laptop (or today's generation of tablets) makes it easy for the business traveler to check email, review status of online postings, send résumés, and all the other tasks needed to be performed.

Find places to connect. One of the more interesting recent developments is the widespread availability of high-speed internet connections in hotels. And in many chains it is now included in the basic room rate. Air cards aren't bad, but they aren't cheap and they are still a little slow making the availability of cheap (or free) broadband is a very nice plus. Similarly, coffee shops, and casual dining restaurants increasingly offer free broadband (Panera Bread is an excellent example). It goes without saying that you must be conscious of your passwords and the sites you visit while in those locations. Your information will be far less secure. I wouldn't do any online banking while in a coffee shop.

Flash memory/ key chain memory, etc. While it goes by many names, the small removable memory devices are remarkable little pieces of technology. Use them to keep copies of résumés, cover letters, and presentations,

whatever. I kept a copy of this manuscript on one. Memory prices keep
dropping while the capacity keeps increasing.

Chapter 18 Momentum

Now that your marketing campaign is in full swing, you need to increase the momentum. While our goal is to create thousands of impressions, a vital few individuals may make a key difference in your success. These are the individuals you nominate as references.

There are a number of objectives in choosing references. The first and most obvious goal is obtaining a favorable reference. But a reference for what? Why should a prospective employer believe the reference?

A second and equally important objective is getting a deep understanding of why an employer would check your references. Armed with that, you will insure that the prospective employer gets their reference questions appropriately answered.

Those are the key subtleties to the reference process which you must master.

<u>Wholehearted endorsement</u>

Being a reference is a position of trust. Never ask anyone to be a reference if you think they will have any reservation. In addition to placing them in an awkward situation, you run a serious risk of a less than enthusiastic endorsement.

Everyone knows that when an employer checks references, he expects them to be good, if not glowing. In my experience checking references for candidates, about the best one can do is to gain a little insight into how to work most effectively with the candidate. If a reference comes back sounding lukewarm, I take that as a big red flag on a candidacy. Again, if you have a doubt or concern that a particular individual might give you a C Minus rather than an A Plus, don't use them as a reference.

<u>The higher the better</u>

Let's face it: a reference from Jack Welch, Bill Gates or Warren Buffet is going to go further than a reference from the assistant manager on the night shift at Quickie Mart. If you have influential names as references, by all means use them. But don't use them if they aren't real or if they won't recall who you are without a prompt. You don't want a perspective employer to place a call only to have to explain who you are to your own reference.

<u>Preparation</u>

It is more than just good manners or common courtesy to call someone to get their permission to be a reference; it is essential. You must judge the level of enthusiasm they have for being your reference. Unless your potential reference knows you extremely well, and is very current on your activities and career, you should update them on your most recent activities (including a concise explanation of why you are looking for a new position). Further, inform them as to the kind of position you are seeking. At that point, you should send them a résumé or two and ask for their review and comments.

Periodically let your references know what the status of your job search is. Once every six to eight weeks should be sufficient, and email will usually be appropriate for these updates. Be conscious of the time commitment of your references.

Contact them again if you are a finalist and are you expect the prospective employer to check references. Let your references know the details of the position you are considering, the plusses and minuses, and generally fill them in on the business and organization. References can also play a different but equally valuable role: that of the coach/disciplinarian. That is, the wise counselor who will tell you that a particular position really isn't for you. That's happened to me. As a finalist for a rather well-paid position, I was lining up my references. As I described the job and named the employer to one of my former bosses, who was known for being direct, he began questioning me sharply. He asked why I thought that business had staying power, and in particular what set them apart from their competitors. He pointed out what I knew, but wasn't facing. Prospects for that business weren't rosy. I dropped out of consideration and shortly thereafter found a better and more appropriate position.

Some references need coaching. As an illustration, if your reference knew you as part of a large organization, you may need to give them a coaching comment such as: "I'm a finalist for a database administrator role. As you recall, I held that position for four years back at ABC before I was promoted, so I'm very well qualified."

Even if your reference won't need a prompt, they certainly deserve notification that you have recently given them as a reference, and you expect them to get a call. Describe the job, and any concerns or reservations that you think the employer might have about your qualifications. It is those concerns that the hiring manager will be most interested in vetting. That gives your reference adequate time to reflect on possible answers and guidance for the hiring manager.

<u>Different positions, different references</u>

This is a lost opportunity for many, if not most, job seekers. Let's say you have eight years of experience in manufacturing, eight in chemical processing and eight in services. If you are a finalist for a services position, doesn't it make sense to have a service industry reference or two? Just as we have said to tailor both your résumé and your cover letter or email, tailor your references.

<u>References are networking contacts too</u>

Contacting potential references to seek their permission sets off a chain of events. Former bosses and coworkers may know of current openings. They may have secretly hoped you could join them in their current positions. Or, they may want you back at an old employer. Or they may know of a position elsewhere. This, however, remains a secondary, not a primary motivation for contacting them.

It is fair to ask them to be on the lookout for a position that they believe would be right for you. If they ask for specifics, be prepared. If they volunteer to help further, by all mean take advantage of it. But honor this trust: you want them to stand up for you when their phone rings with a hiring employer on the other end.

<u>Why do references get checked anyway?</u>

In a time when many corporate policies require limiting disclosures to the dates of employment, why do prospective employers even bother?

There are a several reasons. First, is important to establish that a prospect worked where he said he did, in the job title he said he had, since some candidates are given to exaggeration in their résumé's claims. Second, the skillful questioner may learn a little more than name rank and serial number. And third, to ask the reference for the name of someone else. When I'm checking references that is my key goal: obtain the name of someone else to contact other than the names supplied to me by the candidate. I'm not always successful in that endeavor, but when I am, I believe I've increased the odds of talking to someone who will be more likely to share some constructive comments, or even a negative comment. After all, no one hands out the names of someone for a reference who they believe will say something terrible about them. So, whenever I can, I try to get at least one reference that the candidate didn't provide. Assume that I'm not the only one who does this-your next prospective employer may be trolling for another person to quiz about you.

Be aware then, that the best interviewers (who generally are the kind of person you want for a supervisor) are likely to try to find additional individuals to validate your skills and weaknesses. Are there employers in your past that you would just as soon not come up? Then it is important to not only exclude them, but also exclude anyone else from that firm if there is any chance they might help a hiring manager talk to someone at that firm who will be sharply negative on your performance. If the prospective employer is going to turn that reference up, let it be a result of superior diligence and detective work on their part. You have no duty to make their job easier in that regard.

In Larry Bossidy and Ram Charan's bestselling business book *Execution*, there is a section on hiring strong performers with a history of getting things done versus individuals who talk a good game but disappoint when it comes down to getting results. Mr. Bossidy describes many of the questions he uses in assessing candidates. These questions focus on energy, enrolling others in achievement and decisiveness. As you think of references to give in particular circumstances, you must decide what the hiring manager is most concerned about. Is it a Bossidy, looking for energy and results? Or is it a more technical position, and the interviewer is making sure that you really do know how to use Java and Perl, and have lead an SAP implementation?

The references you provide should be the ones best qualified to address those questions on your behalf.

Chapter 19 Preparation

Your army is advancing. Thousands of résumés are in the air. Geometric power is driving your network. Your website is getting hundreds of hits. The résumés that you have posted on various websites are getting noticed.

Suddenly the phone rings, or the email pings–finally, a contact from the one employer that you have been working so hard to get! Now you have landed the interview with a company that has a position of great interest. Your accumulated skill and experience must help you to defeat the younger and less experienced opponent. In this chapter, you make final preparations to go mano-a-mano.

The degree and quality of preparation for that first interview is critical in determining whether you make it into further discussions and get an offer. So, we are going to polish you to a deep sheen.

Objective: make it to second round interviews, or get an offer during the first round. Or, if your meeting is with an executive recruiter, getting the recruiter to pass the intelligence he has gathered about you on to his client with a recommendation that the client meet you.

Tactic one: conduct superior reconnaissance and information gathering.

<u>Preparation for meeting with an employer</u>

The depth and breadth of information available on a company varies widely depending on size, public versus private and industry. However, for the thoughtful researcher, amazing amounts of information are available. Information can be found:

- In government filings
- On corporate web sites
- In the definitely NOT corporate web sites
- Chatrooms/message boards
- The local library
- By primary research
- Public records

<u>Government filings</u>

For public companies, the first stop is the EDGAR database within the Securities and Exchange Commission's files (www.sec.gov/edgar/searchedgar/) . I am amazed at how few serious job candidates access this treasure trove of information. Every US publicly traded company must file quarterly and annual reports, (10Q's and 10K's respectively) and annual proxy statements. Further, any time a company issues initial or additional stock or publicly traded bonds, it must file a registration statement, known as an S-1 or S-14. And, under today's infamous Reg FD world (Full Disclosure regulation) companies frequently file presentations to investors and other important recent developments on form 8-K.

Every one of those documents contains a rich mine of information. If you are pursuing an opportunity with a public company and are seriously interested in it, you simply must spend time reviewing the EDGAR database. Study the annual reports, making sure that you carefully read the Management Discussion and Analysis ("MD&A") section that describes the change in the business from previous years to the most recent. While "risk factors", which are things that could go wrong and reduce the value of the business and thereby harm investors used to be found only in registration statements, increasingly, companies are listing risk factors in quarterly (Form 10-Q) and annual (Form 10-K) reports. Risk factors may provide an excellent source of material for developing questions for your prospective employer.

Study the footnotes carefully. If you are a non-financial type and find yourself lost in accounting jargon and technical topics, get someone you know with a financial background to help. And don't let it bother you that some of this stuff is hard to understand: I'm a CPA and I find the accounting for taxes, pensions and derivatives to be arcane and hard to understand myself.

And, obviously you should review the financial statements. Calculate some ratios like:

- Debt to equity. (Take total debt that pays interest; divide that by total shareholders' equity. Shareholders' equity is always found at the

bottom of the balance sheet. If the balance sheet is shown on two pages, it will be at the bottom of the right).
- EBIT margin (Earnings Before Interest and Taxes divided by Sales)
- Return on Equity (Net Income divided by Shareholders' Equity), and
- Return on Total Capital (Net Income plus after tax Interest Expense, divided by Shareholders' Equity plus total interest-bearing debt) [14]

for all periods presented. Are the ratios improving or has economic performance slipped (or worse?). Again, financial performance and MD&A can provide fertile ground for devising interview questions.

The proxy statement discloses the compensation of the highest paid officers. If you are a candidate for an executive position, this is the place to learn how you might be compensated versus your peers, or if the compensation is interesting at all. Further, the proxy provides insight into stock ownership by insiders. Look at this carefully-it can be particularly useful in identifying key family ownership positions, controlling interests, or a member of management whose influence is potentially greater than indicated by his title because of the amount of stock he owns. It generally will also describe any employment agreements held by insiders and any transactions between the company and insiders. Further, it lists all the board members. On two occasions, I've known board members of companies I was interested in! That connection is too valuable to overlook.

The proxy will also disclose employment agreements. If this is relevant to your potential employment, those agreements are almost always filed at some point as part of a proxy or other document which will be available on the SEC website.

Review form 8-K for current developments. If you find a PowerPoint presentation to investors, you've struck gold! The executive management teams of companies periodically prepare these promotional documents to present to large institutional investors (that is, portfolio managers for mutual funds, pension funds, insurance companies, hedge funds and the like) and to Wall Street financial analysts. These presentations generally describe the company's business strategy and growth plans. This provides you the opportunity to get a robust view of how your skills might match the company's direction, and to prepare your message so that you convey that mutuality of interests in a highly effective way.

<u>Trade publications</u>

The depth and breadth of industries covered by trade publications is simply remarkable. If you are committed to remaining in your current field, you should certainly subscribe to the leading publications covering your industry. In addition to keeping you current on developments, and frequently providing insight into company strategy, you will see the organization changes announced. Every trade publication I know of highlights important executive and management changes. Frequently, there is a section listing all the announced job moves. This can both identify immediate opportunities and locate former associates. Many of the publications run classified employment ads. Even if none of those ads are for positions of interest, you get insight into companies that are hiring.

Over the years, I've been a subscriber to:

<u>Information Week</u>

<u>Chain Store News</u>

<u>Drug Store News</u>

<u>The Jeweler's Circular Keystone</u>

<u>CRM</u>

<u>Garden Center Business</u>

<u>CFO</u>

<u>Restaurant News</u>

<u>Kitchen and Bath News</u>

<u>Computer Reseller News</u>

<u>The Journal of Accountancy</u>

<u>PC Magazine</u>   [15]

<u>Home Furnishings News</u>

<u>Industry Week</u>

<u>The Manufacturer</u>

<u>The Deal</u>

<u>Financial Executive</u>

And many others.

If you are interviewing outside of industries you have worked in before, finding and reading some trade journals is one of the fastest and most effective ways to get a grasp of competitors, trends, key players and so on in an industry. Make a trip to your local library and ask a librarian to help you. I've found them amazingly knowledgeable and helpful.

<u>Corporate Web Site</u>

Spend extensive time on your target's web site. In addition to studying the content, look at the style, technique and purpose. Is the site designed to conduct ecommerce transactions, or establish a presence and image? Are the look, logo, advertising and feel of the site the same as in other media, or is it different? Are job openings listed? *What are they?* These provide great insight into where the company's needs are, how it is expanding, etc.

For many technology companies, particularly in the business-to-business area, websites present case studies of the product or service in use. These qualify for detailed study.

Most companies post their press releases on their website–another extremely valuable source of information. Study these carefully, going back as far as possible. Note financial results and commentary and financial presentations.

Pay particular attention to personnel announcements. Is the position you are seeking one that was filled a mere year ago, and a year prior to that? Uh Oh. Are the press releases current, or were there flurries of releases two years ago, a few from one year ago, and none posted this year? Probably means performance has deteriorated, funding has dried up, or new products aren't being introduced at the same rate.

Is the web site being well-maintained, or is the content stale, and links broken?

The standard for presentations on the web has emerged. Common terms are "About Us" "Investors" or "Investor Relations". Any section like that should be reviewed carefully. Many companies now publish profiles of their key executives on the corporate site. Look for "Management Team". Make absolutely sure that you check out those profiles. The investor section also may contain the same reports filed with the SEC, along with press releases, and again, possibly copies of investor presentations. This may well include an audio track that accompanies the company's slide show, and even possibly a video presentation.

This cumulative information can help provide some subtle insights into the company.

<u>The Definitely NOT Company Web Site</u>

Many large companies, particularly ones that have done mass layoffs or downsizing, generate a lot of disgruntled employees. In the new millennium, disgruntled employees create [company name] sucks.com, or .net, or former [company name].com. Savvy companies now register these when registering their domain name. If you find these, they may well provide some interesting counter perspective to the positive image the company attempts to project.

<u>Primary research</u>

For certain kinds of businesses directly touching end-user customers, like retailing or restaurants, there is no substitute for conducting first-person, or primary, research. Shop the store, eat at the restaurant, stay in the hotel, ride the bike, test the software, well, you get the picture. However, every good researcher will tell you about the criticality of sample size. You are a sample of one; don't let one location in a chain dominate your thinking–you are far too experienced to make that mistake. Rather, it is one data element in a chain of information you are connecting.

During my last search for a new position, I was a candidate for CFO of a large, publicly traded jewelry retail company. Let's call it Newco. While I had been in retail jewelry before, it was fifteen years ago (!) Needless to say my information and context was stale. In addition to reviewing the financial information, I began visiting the company's stores. I put on my full combat dress: navy suit and crisply ironed white shirt, and asked to see the store manager at each one. I told the manager that I was a candidate for a position with the company at the headquarters office. In EVERY case the manager spent extensive time with me, giving me details about likes and dislikes, the technology employed, corporate programs and management style. In discussions at one store, after learning of my previous employer those fifteen years before, the manager asked me if I knew Mr. X from that time. When I replied that I did indeed know Mr. X, he immediately told me that Mr. X now worked for Newco, at a nearby location!

The following week, Mr. X and I renewed acquaintance, and he gave me two hours full of invaluable information. Of all the candidates interviewing for that position, do you think any went to the corporate office to interview better prepared than I was?

Somewhere in the web of connections you identified in Chapter 3 are people who know your target company first hand. Using LinkedIn and emailing some of your lists is generally the fastest way to find them. A simple message of: "I'm looking for some information on Company Z, where I believe there is an opportunity. Do you know them, or can you refer me to someone who does?" will get the job done. While you are awaiting those replies, develop a list of five pieces of information about the company, management and the specific opportunity that you would like to know more about. When a reply comes in, quickly follow-up. Be honest and specific about the job you are a candidate for, and obtain all the data you can. A phone call is probably the most efficient way to get these answers. Of course, you simply must send a thank you card and an offer to reciprocate to anyone taking the time to help you.

Insider tip: entering the business name in the search bar for LinkedIn will yield a list of every employee at that firm who is registered with LinkedIn. For some larger firms that is a list of thousands! If the list isn't overwhelming, you can scan it to see if there is someone you know employed there. LinkedIn will also indicate connections-that is, someone you are connected with is connected with someone at your targeted firm. The becomes another source of company information.

The Library

As previously discussed, public libraries have become the center of job searches. Many larger cities have dedicated business libraries, with librarians who are remarkably talented. Research the industry's size and growth. The US Statistical Abstract is usually a great place to start, and every library has one. Use the library's capabilities to identify the trade publications just discussed.

Librarians can also help identify and locate those trade publications to help you with industry background.

Libraries now generally have high-speed Internet access to help with you search. And, libraries generally have access to subscription services which feature fast and powerful information gathering and search features, like Hoovers and the Wall Street Journal online.

The Stock Broker

Do you have a brokerage account? If so, see if your brokerage firm covers either the company or the industry your target company is in. Brokerage firms hire exceptionally smart and talented individuals to research industries and companies and prepare recommendations for their clients. Some firms call them analysts, others research analysts, and still others financial analysts. Many analysts are true experts. For example, some of the analysts who follow pharmaceutical and medical device companies are Medical Doctors (M.D.'s). Some analysts following semiconductor or microprocessor manufacturers are engineers. They know their stuff.

Call your broker or go to your online account and obtain that research and study it carefully. Use the work product of these experts to learn industry trends, which firms they see winning and losing, insight into financial performance and sometimes just some good management gossip.

<u>Preparation for meeting with a recruiter</u>

Here the task is more difficult, and the data less robust. Nonetheless preparation is essential.

Just as in preparing for a company meeting, visit the recruiter's website. Even the smallest recruiter is likely to have a site, and the larger executive search firms have a significant internet presence. Absorb everything you can about the firm. Is the individual you are meeting with high in the firm–generally indicated by titles like "partner", "managing director" or "global practice area leader", or at the bottom, usually "associate"?.

Use the search engines like Google, Yahoo, and Bing to see if you can learn anything more about the individual recruiter. Check also for a LinkedIn page on the recruiter.[16] Every piece of data can prove valuable.

In Chapter 12 we covered the basic steps when a recruiter calls. These are essential when preparing for a meeting with a recruiter. The most important step involves the job description, or "job spec". You *must* get the spec and compare your skills and background carefully against that description. I make detailed notes in the margin of each area where I have directly relevant background or a significant accomplishment. While the primary purpose of this exercise is preparation to prove to the recruiter that you are an eminently qualified candidate, there is an equally important goal. It is to insure that you really are a great candidate, and that the position interests you. At this point in your career, you cannot afford a mistake or wasted time. If you aren't qualified or interested, withdraw now. Don't waste your time or the recruiter's–a good recruiter will respect you for it.

As an experienced individual, you should also examine the job description for what *isn't* there–it frequently is more significant that what is. For example, if you are an experienced CIO and you are reviewing a job description that doesn't say anything about application development, an alarm should go off. If application development doesn't report to the CIO, to whom does it report? Isn't that reporting structure unusual? Isn't it likely to create issues? When you have that meeting with the recruiter, ask why the CIO's responsibilities don't include that important category.

Tactic two: Preparing your questions.

Just as the interviewers at the company you are about to visit are organizing their favorite, toughest questions, you too must prepare yours. These should, in large part, reflect the information garnered and the issues identified in your research. Just like your list of accomplishments, you need at least twenty questions. Generally, five to ten on the specific position and ten to fifteen on the company would be a good mix.

Recently I was a candidate for an executive position with a specialty chemical company. I studied and analyzed corporate performance, reviewed all recent public filings, found an individual I knew on their board and talked to him, found a friend of the CEO and talked to him; found an old associate working for their auditors and quizzed him; in short I was very well prepared and rehearsed. The CEO was indeed generous in his time commitment to me— we spent over two hours together. When I got the green light to ask questions, I began to fire away from my prepared list. Generally I'm able to engage CEO's in lengthy discussions of strategy, competitors, competitive advantage, culture and so on, but not this time. He gave very short answers to all my questions. We covered my twenty in less than twenty minutes! Now I take pains to have thirty or even forty questions…

I've included some sample questions on Exhibit 19-1. However, it is critical to tailor the questions around the specifics of the company, the industry, the position and your interests. Did your research show that sales are more robust, or less robust, than competitors? Ask why. Does the position you are considering seem to be one that a well-managed company generally can fill internally? Why couldn't they? Did the research show that the company introduced new products or opened new locations? How are those performing? How is the company organized–by geography, by customer type, or by product line? Where will growth come from?

When I interview candidates, the quality and thoughtfulness of their questions is a critical determinant of how I view them.

Exhibit 19-1-Sample Interview Questions-Employer

The Company

- What are the top three or four objectives for the company for this year?
- How has the business strategy of the company changed in the last two years?
- Who do you view as your most effective competitors? Why?
- What is the basis for competition–service, price, new products, design and style, etc.?
- What changes do you anticipate in the industry and the market in the next few years?
- Describe the culture the company is creating and maintaining.
- How is your financial performance versus competitors?
- What are the most important trends in the industry?
- Different companies use different processes to run the business–for example–some use monthly reviews and an annual budget, others use strategic plans and weekly management meetings. What are the key processes the company uses to run the business?
- What is the role of technology in the business? Are there important new technologies in the industry?
- What kinds of market segments are there? Which are the most important? Which are the fastest growing?
- How is performance evaluated within the company?

The Position

- Why is this position open?
- What are the key objectives of this position?
- How will performance be measured?
- (If this is a management position) what is the quality of the direct reports to this position?
- How do they feel about this position being filled from the outside?

The Culture

- If you think about employees that were hired into the company at management levels as opposed to promoted from within, are there any common attributes of those who have been successful?

- Are there common attributes of those who have not been successful?
- If you think about defense contractors run by ex-military command and control style companies as one end of the spectrum, and Internet companies where employees bring their pets to work as the other end of the cultural spectrum, where does your company fit?
- If you could change something about the culture, what would it be?
- What is healthy and powerful about the culture you would like to have the organization embrace even more?

The Process

- What process is the company using to identify and select the eventual employee?
- What is the timetable? Ideally, when would you want this position filled?
- What kind of training and orientation will the successful candidate receive?

As an interviewer, the quality and thoughtfulness of the questions I received when talking to candidates was a critical component of how I ranked candidates. Did the questions indicate thoughtfulness about the opportunity? Had they done some smart research? Were they good listeners and observers?

If you are unemployed, you have no excuse for not doing good research and developing informed questions. Not only will the questions help separate you from other candidates, more importantly, the questions help you decide whether or not to accept an offer if one is forthcoming.

Some of the best decisions I've ever made were turning down job offers–*including turning one down while I was unemployed with not very many opportunities coming my way.*

<u>Job description</u>

If you've been furnished a copy of the position description (and I would have some concerns about the company if you haven't) match your skills, background and accomplishments to the requirements of the job. I generally use a highlighter on key points on the position, and make margin notes where I have particularly relevant experience or skills.

In the next chapter, we'll cover the final preparation for your interview

Chapter 20 The Interview

It's show time!

You've gotten up, worked out, had your breakfast, checked the newspaper and television for any big news or developments that everyone will be talking about.

You've left your home or hotel with adequate time to allow for traffic delays. You've got some extra résumés printed on bond paper for anyone who has an illegible copy. All the work you've done is going to pay off. Let's walk through each step.

<u>The last minute check</u>

When you arrive at the company, go to the rest room for that last minute look in the mirror and rest break. You are in shape, informed, practiced, drilled and rehearsed, and ready to go mano-a-mano or mujer-a-mujer!

<u>Meeting conduct</u>

If you are one of the rare and lucky individuals who has worked for your last employer for a number of years, you may be rusty on the art of interviewing. If you have followed all the steps to this point, you are in excellent shape, but here are a few reminders:

<u>The introduction</u>

Some employers use a team approach to interviewing. A number of individuals meet a candidate for an hour or more each. First impressions are indeed important, so:

- Offer your hand first and always give your name, e.g."Hi, I'm Scott Kreger".
- Look the person you are greeting directly in the eyes. If you have any doubt that you will remember her name–then repeat it back to her. Since you are going to use her name in follow-up notes (as described later in this chapter), clarify any spelling at that moment, which will also help fix the name in your mind, e.g. is that Cathy with a "C" or

Kathy with a "K"?
- Remain standing until you are invited to sit.
- Look around the room for anything that will give you a conversation starter with the interviewer, such as a trophy for the company softball team, a Six-Sigma diploma, family pictures at the beach, or the latest business book. Each of these can be used to establish rapport or cover "dead air" during your discussions, e.g. "I see you read Clay Christensen's most recent book. How did you like it?"

Meeting control

The interviewing manager is clearly in charge, and you must let them ask questions initially. However, you are interviewing the company as much as they are interviewing you. Typical first round interviews are about an hour. Generally, I recommend that you give the first fifteen minutes solely to the employer for his questions. Somewhere between fifteen to thirty minutes is a good time to begin to asking some of your questions. This requires the use of your judgment and an actor's sense of timing. Use their questions to introduce yours. For example, if the firm has been asking you about how advertising expenses were budgeted and managed in your last position, once you have answered the question, introduce yours. "While we are on the topic of developing and managing an advertising budget, how does that process work here? When will you start developing next year's plan?" This enables a more robust interview, and should provide you with valuable information for other interviews with other managers or second-round meetings with the same individual.

Avoid at all costs

There are some topics you just do not want to introduce or areas that are out of bounds:

- Religion. (Unless you are interviewing for a position with a church).
- Politics. (Unless you are interviewing with a lobbying firm).
- Employee benefit plans. You will have plenty of opportunities to analyze the benefits plan once they have made you an offer.
- Vacation time. Nothing turns me off faster than an inquiry about our vacation program on a first interview. It makes me feel that they don't

have the right level of interest and professionalism.

- Profanity. I once interviewed a candidate for a critical, senior level executive position. I'm no prude, and I've been known to get salty myself, but his use of profanity was simply shocking, and all the more so since this was our initial meeting. I couldn't help but wonder what his conversation would be like if he were part of our company and was comfortable around us. If he would use that language with (essentially) strangers, what would it be like if he knew us well?

Energy

Demonstrate energy. I'm a rather low-key individual. That, however, doesn't mean that I'm not very competitive and achievement oriented. One of the lessons I've had to learn personally during the recent downturn (yes, I was unemployed for quite some time), was how many hiring managers are looking for a demonstration of energy, activity and passion. Since I advanced through a technical specialty, when interviewing candidates I have generally focused on technical skills and capability, and not so much on passion, commitment and energy. However, I've come to realize that many employers look for signs of highly energetic new employees.

I've long been a member of a networking group. This group welcomes job leads from executive recruiters, which are posted on its website for out-of-work members. Members tend to be older; I would guess forty-five and up, with the preponderance in their fifties. I had an executive recruiter call with a specific position he was seeking to fill. I volunteered to pass it along to my networking group. He declined, noting that he had tried our group before, and the applicants were older, with little drive, just looking for a paycheck until retirement. While I feel strongly that his assessment was erroneous, and that, indeed, frequently older workers with a new job feel like they have something to prove and will often out produce their younger counterparts. Nonetheless, his perception remains. And it is the bias and misperceptions of individuals like him that you must overcome.

One senior executive I know well, who has extensive experience managing sales executives, many of whom make over $300,000 per year, selects new talent largely on his perception of their drive and energy. This, of course, isn't easy to demonstrate as a candidate–but your smile, handshake, preparation, and level of attention during the interview go a long way to indicate energy and determination.

Answer the question asked

Some individuals seem to struggle with delivering good crisp answers. Perhaps they are anxious, having been out of work for an extended period. Perhaps they just aren't comfortable in the give and take of an interview. Whatever the reason, this trait will severely limit their opportunities. As an example, I interviewed an experienced manager for a Director position with six figure compensation. We established a good quick rapport. I asked him to describe his key accomplishments in his last couple of positions–a question he should have answered with a concise, quantified, thoughtful answer. Instead, I got a rambling response that described some job history, some accomplishments and some responsibilities. It became a long monolog. He talked himself out of first place among the candidates we had seen!

Since you have developed your accomplishments and listed them in your résumé, developed your fact list, and practiced answering questions, this will not be your fate. You know to always answer the question asked, give good thoughtful answers, framed in sound bites. If your interviewer isn't satisfied with your answer, they will ask a follow-up.

The Traveler's Checklist

Is this interview out of town? Here is a checklist to make sure that you pack everything you are going to need. You should be relaxed and confident when going to the interview, not scrambling because you forgot your belt.

Men's checklist

Personal grooming

- Toothbrush
- Toothpaste
- Dental floss
- Razor (or electric razor)
- Razor blades

- · Shaving cream
- · Power supply for electric razor
- · Aftershave
- · Mouthwash
- · Hair brush
- · Hair spray
- · Deodorant
- · Shampoo
- · Styptic pencil–no razor cuts with little pieces of tissue stuck on them.

<u>Men – apparel</u>

- · Suit: Charcoal gray or navy, or charcoal gray or navy pinstripe
- · White or blue shirt (If you plan to wear a shirt with French cuffs, cufflinks)
- · Tie
- · Belt
- · Socks
- · Dress shoes
- · Shoe shine cloth
- · Underwear
- · Handkerchief
- · Collar stays
- · Exercise outfit: running shoes, shorts, tee shirt and athletic socks

<u>Women – grooming</u>

- · Foundation
- · Lipstick
- · Eye shadow
- · Eye liner
- · Cold cream
- · Shampoo
- · Hair brush
- · Hair spray
- · Deodorant
- · Toothbrush
- · Toothpaste

- Mouthwash
- Dental Floss

<u>Women-apparel</u>

- Dress or suit: black or navy
- Blouse or shirt: white or blue
- Underwear
- Bra
- Pantyhose (OK, this may be passé; use your own judgment after studying the firm you're meeting)
- Dress shoes
- Shoe shine cloth
- Belt
- Exercise outfit: running shoes, shorts, tee shirt and athletic socks

<u>Both</u>

- Smart phone
- Laptop or tablet
- Chargers

<u>Both men and women</u>

Bring a spare shirt, blouse and tie. Accidents happen. Don Bolen, the retired former president of USAA insurance, kept a crisply starched and pressed white shirt in his car and office at all times in case something happened, or even if he felt his activities during the day had left him appearing unkempt. I never saw Don when he didn't look professional. Don't let that spilled cup of coffee knock you off stride. Have that security blanket nearby.

Take your smartphone, and make sure that the company has your cell number in case they need to make last minute contact.

Finally, organize your documents: business cards, résumés, itinerary, company address and contact numbers. I have a place in my bag that I always place my itinerary, and I always put my airline tickets in my coat breast pocket. I use colored transparent plastic folders to organize all my materials inside of my messenger bag. It both protects the contents and makes things easy to find. You don't want to be fumbling through your Tumi bag to find a résumé while a potential employer is watching.

<u>Last minute cramming</u>

Before the interview, you need your last cram session to get key data back in short term memory and quickly accessible, and to make sure you have smooth, natural-sounding answers to those key questions from Chapter 19.

So, if you are not having dinner with the company the night before, use that time to review:

- Your accomplishments.
- Your response to "I've seen your résumé but tell me about yourself".
- The key numbers in your résumé, e.g. the number of people managed, dollars of budget you were responsible for, savings realized, sales generated and so on. You want those facts and figures at your immediate recall.

Insiders tip: if this is an out-of town interview, and you have the option to come in the night before, take it. With new airport security, risk of bad weather, bankrupt airlines, and hotels that will overbook, give yourself the extra time. If anything goes wrong, you have time to adjust without feeling rushed.

If you have traveled for this interview, press your shirt or blouse after you check in to your room. I know, it sounds stupid, but I now do it regularly. After all, I'm not a teenager, and I want to look as good as possible. Most all hotels now routinely put an ironing board and an iron in the room. Press your clothes while watching a business channel like CNBC, or while watching the news. You don't want to be the only candidate not aware of some developing story.[17]

Eat a light dinner and don't have anything more than a single glass of wine to drink. And here is that reminder from Chapter 3: check for all that hair that shouldn't be there– nose, ears, legs, etc. Check immediately upon entering your hotel room since you might need time to find a store with tweezers or clippers if airline security confiscated yours.

Go to bed early and get a good night's sleep. After all, you are the old pro and can easily handle this situation.

<u>The morning</u>

Get up REALLY early. You are going to exercise as normal. (You might casually mention during the interview process that the hotel had a nice exercise area, or that you jogged even though it was a bit chilly, as part of your youth propaganda).

Then you are going to shower, get dressed, have a light, healthy breakfast and review the newspapers for anything that might be relevant for your day, and to make sure that you have the topical knowledge for any water cooler conversation that might occur. Be sure to check the local sports pages for what is going on there: the odds of you meeting a sports nut during the interview process are high.

I would say "good luck" but you don't need it. You are ready!

Chapter 21 Dinner

The savviest companies want to see a job candidate in a social setting. These are exceptionally treacherous situations, and you must be on guard every second.

There are two kinds of dinner interviews. The first type occurs early in the process when a hiring manager arranges a one-on-one dinner. Anything could have triggered it–ranging from the manager simply being in the same town as the candidate on a business trip and is making good use of his time, all the way to a dinner that is the last step before a job offer.

The second is the group dinner. It is also exceptionally dangerous for the candidate: one slip by you *or your spouse* and you are out. The invitation to the group dinner is however, very good news: it is usually the last hurdle before getting an offer. The time and money for a group dinner interview is usually only reserved for the first place candidate. To succeed, you need to know what their objectives are, and you must demonstrate the skills of Henry Kissinger at a dinner for the Chinese Premier, coupled with the style of Miss Manners.

Let's examine each in detail. First, the one-on-one dinner. The one-on-one dinner must be placed in the context of the interview process. If this is an initial meeting, then it is simply an interview, plus a chance to see the candidate in a social setting. If however, a retained search firm is involved (see Chapter 20), something more encouraging may be involved. For example, the recruiter may have told the hiring manager that he has found an outstanding candidate with great matching skills, and that the hiring manager should move quickly. Or, if the position you are interested in is in the local branch of a multi-location business, it might be simply that the hiring manager is coming to the candidates, rather than the candidates coming to him.

In any case, you should prepare like any other interview (Chapters 19-20) but in addition you must exhibit table manners that demonstrate that you've learned correct business and dining etiquette as you were maturing. Given the widespread ignorance and weak upbringing of many younger applicants today, this should give you a clear advantage. If you need a refresher on

forks, spoons, placement, etc., there are several good ones on
www.youtube.com . I recommend the one by Laurah Amy-fun and
informative (Use the search feature at youtube to find it easily).

The types of organizations that will want to see you in action socially are
usually very smart businesses. Smart enough to manage multiple objectives at
the same time. These dinners usually have a group of two to four couples.
These will include at least one of the individuals who interviewed you, but
also usually include some new players–probably would-be peers to your
prospective new position. Someone is likely there to:

- Judge your spouse's reaction to everything–is the spouse opposed
  to the move or the new job?
- See how you react to a social setting–are you relaxed and
  comfortable?
- Learn if you are outgoing and can carry a conversation.
- Find if you say too much about your current or a previous
  employer.
- Observe if you tend to be too negative about a previous employer.
- Have important skills and background that hasn't come up in an
  interview.
- Have an experience or background weakness that hasn't come up
  in an interview.

These events tend to follow a predictable agenda, particularly if you must
relocate for the position. It will be something like: Day 1 (frequently a
Friday), standard interviews in the office for the candidate; house-hunting trip
for the spouse. Day 2, candidate and spouse continue house hunting; a brief
trip back to the hotel for cleaning-up, then off to dinner.

*Insider tip one: if the company has arranged a realtor to organize a market
overview and a house-hunt, assume that the realtor is in on the game and will
let the company know anything and everything that is said….*

Here then are some do's and don'ts of the dinner interview.

<u>Etiquette</u>

At every stage, demonstrate a working knowledge of etiquette as well as common sense.

- Men always open doors–including car doors–for women.
- Men hold the chair for a woman to sit.
- Guests wait for the host to sit.
- Candidates follow the host's lead in ordering alcohol, and always order something less potent.
- Never, *NEVER* have too much to drink. If you are stupid enough to have more than two drinks in an interview dinner, you don't deserve to get a new job.
- While dining, keep one hand in your lap unless you are cutting something or serving something.
- No elbows or forearms on the table: you are not guarding or protecting anything.
- OK-I've already covered smoking. If you are a smoker, you are a non-smoker during this event if you have to have three Nicoderm patches to make it.

<u>Prepared answers</u>

Assume that you will have a very predictable series of questions that you and your spouse will have to answer. If this position involves relocating, there will be lots of questions and conversation about that. Have your answers down pat. You and your spouse should even practice a little on the trip to the interview, or at the hotel.

- What interested you in this position?
- How did your housing hunting trip go? "OH MY GOD HOUSES HERE ARE INCREDIBLY EXPENSIVE FOR TINY LITTLE PIECES OF JUNK" may be what you want to say, but you can't. "We had a productive day with (___ name of realtor). He really knows the area and is taking good care of us" is the right answer.
- How do your children feel about the move? (You may well have an age advantage here–because your children are grown and you don't have to worry about new schools, transferring grades, finding a pediatrician and the like).
- What activities are your children involved in?

· What do you like to do for fun?

Assume that the hiring manager will get a report on everything that happened, what was done and what was said promptly the next morning.

And, you owe the host a thank-you note when you return home.

Chapter 22 Mopping Up

"Everything with my command was successful in the highest degree" General *William Sherman*

My uncle, the late Sergeant William "Bill" Sanders was a decorated WWII veteran who saw action in the Asian theater including the legendary battle of Luzon in the Philippines. Uncle Bill used to say that he and his men could handle almost anything except being told that all that was left was a "mopping up" exercise. Their experience was that casualties ran high while "mopping up".

In competing with younger job applicants, you will find that in the mopping up stage you can lose out on a good job opportunity as well.

A good time to begin your follow-up to an interview is when you are leaving the building or turning off the video conference (!)

If you developed a thorough list of questions and were able to ask them, you have a highly informed view of the process they are going through, and an idea about the date they would like to have the position filled. From here, monitor the calendar and take appropriate action at the right time. It is *critical* not to seem desperate for a new position. In my experience, many highly qualified, capable candidates torpedo their chances in this phase. They have been out of work for a while and have come to realize the difficulties older workers have. They may be in financial difficulty. Their emotions take control, and they clumsily try to close the deal prematurely. If you've been in sales, you know when to ask for the order and when to wait. Appear interested, enthusiastic, but cautious. Realistically, no matter how much you enjoy my book, (and you must have found value to get to Chapter 22) the goal is to get a new position and keep it for a while–not be re-reading this book and searching for the next job in a few months. Therefore, both the job content and the job environment need to be right for you. It must set you up to succeed. As the experienced candidate, you must demonstrate your professionalism and wisdom in this phase, and *explore together with the hiring firm* if this is the right position for you, and if you are a good fit for the company.

<u>Following up with a recruiter-general</u>

If your meeting was with a recruiter, you will probably know exactly where you stand. Recruiters generally let you know if you are a candidate that they intend to present in person. A recruiter will move briskly to get your interview with the company scheduled. (Remember that usually some of their compensation is tied to completion of the search, so they are motivated.) You, then, must periodically check in with the recruiter on meeting times and locations as well as what the recruiter has learned as other candidates are interviewed. You must also be very diligent about travel plans. Confirm every meeting time and every travel step. Nothing gets an interview off to a worse start than the candidate arriving late-or not at all.

<u>Following up with a recruiter post-meeting with the client</u>

If a recruiter is involved, contact him immediately after the interview and give him a brief synopsis of the day, the questions, any surprises, how the "chemistry" felt, and general impressions. Set a time for the recruiter to contact you with feedback from the company. (After a candidate visits a company, the recruiter almost always contacts the candidate before contacting the company). In this environment with so many quality candidates, recruiters have gotten simply horrible about getting back to candidates-try to get a commitment time from the recruiter. That is, be very specific-he'll call with the employer's view on Tuesday the tenth. However, don't assume that just because the recruiter agreed to call that they actually will. Don't get your expectations too high, but you might be lucky and be dealing with an increasingly rare creature–an honorable recruiter.

In that vein, when you call to give the initial feedback to the recruiter, if the receptionist or admin only offers voice mail, politely turn it down and leave your name and number–forcing the recruiter to contact you.

A letter to the company is required. If you had a full day of interviews and met with multiple people, I do not think you must send a letter to all of them. Instead, send a note to the hiring manager, and perhaps one more–the highest ranking person you met, or the human resources professional. The letter should thank them for their time, summarize a few observations on the day, and indicate your interest in further discussions. If you have *absolutely no interest* in the position, and would prefer any range of menial positions than that position with that company, then you should respectfully withdraw from consideration. You don't have the time to waste on a position that you wouldn't take, and neither should you waste a prospective employer's time. They might just contact you in the future with something more appealing.

A reminder: you likely face a younger competitor for the position. Experience matters. As an aware, effective mature adult, you know how to create an effective memorandum. Keep the letter brief, no more than one page. Write it, let it sit for a few hours, then review it. Run spell check and edit carefully–this is absolutely no place for an error. Your memo should highlight one or two critical points where your experience is directly related to a need they have, such as similarities to a situation you've dealt with effectively before, or related industry experience.

The next item of business post-interview is to write down all the information you received during the interview process. (This is why we said you follow-up begins when you leave the building). When I was last looking for work, if I traveled to the interview, I did that on the flight back. If I was exploring a local opportunity, I frequently went to a Starbucks and recorded my notes while they were still fresh in my memory (and I was adequately caffeinated). We have all seen various studies about how little the human brain retains 24 and 48 hours after an event. (And, we no longer have the short-term memory of a teenager, so this is particularly important for us). What questions did they ask? How did they answer your questions? If you met more than one person, what common themes emerged? How did the facility look? How was everyone dressed? Who were the thought leaders? Did they give you any material? If yes, study it carefully. What question did they ask you didn't answer very well? What question did you answer OK, but that you should have knocked out of the park? What were each individual's interests? What items, books, memorabilia in their offices caught your eye? What is the timetable for a decision? Who seemed to be the real decision-maker? Is there a power behind the throne?

You need great documentation of interviews. Carefully organize all the information, including all the materials you gathered from your research activities, your notes, and any feedback you got from a recruiter and file it where you can retrieve it quickly if you hear from the firm again. As days and weeks go by, you want to be able to get back up-to-speed quickly if you hear from the firm, a network contact or the recruiter. If there are additional rounds of interviews, refer back to this information to prepare for future meetings.[18]

The next follow-up item is to report-back and prepare thank-you notes. If a recruiter was involved, after you make your notes, summarize the four or five most important points. Did you sense a real fit? Did you sense their interest? Are you interested? If they would like to offer you a job, what do you need to know more about to make a decision?

If the interview stemmed from networking, you should also summarize key points then call and thank the individual who helped you get the meeting. Follow that up with a written thank you note (yes, I know a note takes longer, but a thank-you email simply is not acceptable).

Next, take a few minutes and do a plusses and minuses of the position. Be as rational as possible. This, of course, may be extremely difficult to do if you've been out of work for a long time, are having problems paying your bills and your spouse is losing patience. Nonetheless, if you are about to take a position with severe drawbacks, stating them clearly to yourself will help you prepare a plan to deal with them. Conversely, if the plusses begin to look like your ideal position, you need to think of ways to keep your candidacy alive without (a) looking desperate, or (b) being a pest.

Finally, if you pass on the position, or if the firm selects another candidate, use this opportunity to build a lasting relationship. As you read business, trade and professional periodicals and see articles or announcements that you think they will find of interest, clip and send it with a brief hand-written note. Contacts created and maintained this way can become relationships that pay future dividends. You are building a big network to last for your entire career.

In our next chapter, we'll discuss alternatives to finding a traditional position.

Chapter 23 Mercenary?

As your hunt for a new, full-time, permanent position continues, you may find an opportunity for a consulting assignment. These can be puzzling challenges–do you stop your full-time search to get some cash flow, get back in a work environment and repair your damaged ego? Or do you continue your full-time, concentrated search? This is an exceptionally difficult question; there are too many variables for an easy, one-size fits-all, answer.

Here are some considerations.

How solid is your current financial position? If you can hold out indefinitely, score one for continuing to look. If you are worried about paying your mortgage, the relief from stress argues for taking it.

What could the temporary position lead to? In a search for a traditional position, this is a critical issue. Many firms use a "temp-to-perm" approach. That is, for those firms, many or even most employees join first on a temporary employee basis. That saves the company money, in that "temp" positions rarely are covered by employee benefits, and it offers regulatory advantages in that dismissing temps usually has no repercussions, while firing permanent employees involves paperwork, concerns about triggering discrimination claims, extended benefit coverage under the COBRA regulations and the like. And both the candidate and the employer get to work with each other to confirm that the position is a mutual fit. Gather information about whether the company uses that approach. A direct approach might even be better: ask if the company occasionally or frequently uses a "temp to perm" approach to adding staff.

How lucrative can this be? Occasionally, opportunities come along to reap unusual financial rewards. Remember Y2K? During that infamous scare, some of my over fifty year old programmer and analyst friends, who had detailed knowledge and understanding of Cobol, Fortran, Assembler and the like had contracting opportunities during which they earned double or triple their previous wage rates. Currently, many of my middle-aged accounting, lawyer and banker friends are billing attractive hourly rates assisting companies with installing new systems, complying with Sarbanes-Oxley or Dodd-Frank requirements, becoming "PCI Compliant" and understanding and applying new SEC regulations. These frequently become two or three year projects. Opportunities like these deserve particularly close examination. Is the firm profitable and growing? Can you network internally and develop some contacts that could lead to a permanent position upon project completion? Or, are there consulting firms assisting on the project that could use your skills on subsequent projects?

How much momentum does your current search have? Is there a realistic opportunity for multiple job offers soon? If you are a veteran of the free agent nation and have had to find work before, and you are confident that you are a finalist for a couple of permanent jobs, and you are sincerely interested in those permanent jobs, you might not want to dilute your energy by project or consulting work.

For many of my over-fifty friends, taking a temporary position has proven to be the best way to rejoin the work force. One of my best friends recently landed a permanent position with compensation solidly in six figures after an eighteen month consulting assignment. The consulting assignment vastly improved his financial position after an extended period out of work. Even if this new job only lasts him two or three years, it will effectively bridge him into retirement age, with attendant social security benefits and ability to tap his IRA's without a penalty, plus he gets to "top off" his 401(k) retirement plan over the next few years. (Reminder: you can contribute $15,000 to a 401(k) plan, plus an additional $7,500 if you are over fifty, which, of course you are….so you can salt away a cool twenty-two grand a year tax deferred. As the commercial says, it's never been a better time to be silver…).

And to be direct, the older you are, the more you should consider a temporary assignment. If you are sixty-seven or better, unless your skills are truly unusual and in very high demand, you are facing a serious challenge finding an old-fashioned, full-time, on the regular payroll, job. You should give very serious consideration if an attractive temp or contractor role presents itself.

Chapter 24 Troop Morale

"Accept the challenges so that you can find the exhilaration of victory." General George S. Patton, Jr.

Troops at the front too long develop battle fatigue. The pressure of constant vigilance creates a variety of seemingly minor ailments, aches and pains that cumulatively create real health problems. Long hours diminish effectiveness.

And, since you are older than most of the other troops at the front, this effort is going to wear you down faster.

Commanding officers know that relief, shore leave, rotation, "R&R", and weekend passes are critical to maintaining an effective fighting force. You too must plan and schedule activities that reduce the stress level that comes from being out of work, placing cold calls, working long hours, worrying about shrinking savings, mounting bills, how to meet future obligations, or moving from a warm, friendly and supportive place to somewhere new where you don't know a soul. And the dozens of other issues that come from a career transition.

You must face this head-on, like the well-trained and equipped soldier that you now are. Here are some recommendations on actions to restore and maintain your vitality. Everything here is both common-sense and supported by numerous scientific studies.

Objective: repair and reinvigorate all your systems

To do this, we are going to employ a variety of techniques. (One of the most important is the one we've already covered; exercise has more benefits than we can list.)

Tactic one: Give yourself time off. Celebrate every official holiday as you did when you were employed. As you've learned by now, finding a new position is an intense process. Take time with your family and friends to relax, get your mind off this project and onto other things. Plan this carefully to get the most of each Memorial Day, Fourth of July, Labor Day, Thanksgiving, Christmas and Presidents' Day. There aren't that many of them.

Tactic two: Meditation, yoga, stretching, etc. Just like exercise, there are lots of reasons to believe that deep breathing, quite meditation, yoga, relaxation therapy and their many cousins generate tremendous benefits including lowered heart rates, improved better blood pressure, and improved lymph system function. Recently, I've been diagnosed with high blood pressure. I'm really unhappy about it. I've been doing some Zen exercises–trying to do it once per day. If I check my blood pressure before and after (10-15 minutes) I generally find a drop in both systolic and diastolic pressure of 15 points or so.

I'm a believer in deep breathing. Whenever I feel myself getting too stressed, I take just a few minutes–three or four will do the job, and breath really deeply, starting at the bottom of my abdomen and then completely filling my lungs. Hold for a count or two and then exhale slowly and completely. I concentrate on forcing out all the air in my lungs, emptying them, and then slowly inhaling again. This way fresh oxygen gets deep into your lungs, where perhaps some stale air has been. This in turn charges your blood cells with a larger quantity of good fresh oxygen. Doesn't that sound like a good idea? Check this website: http://zenhabits.net for some related ideas.

Tactic three: Go to church[19]. Regularly. Research suggests that people who regularly attend church live longer. And, for those of us who believe that this life is just the warm-up act anyway, the payoff will be immeasurable. A little prayer is a good thing too.

Tactic four: Lean on your family. Confide the ups and downs with your spouse. Talk to your parents, brother, sister, some relative. You need some reassurance and there is no better place to get it.

Tactic five: Write in a journal. This is a surprising technique. Just missed out on a great opportunity? Finished second for a job that was perfect? Still trying to understand why you really lost the last position? Spend a few minutes writing what happened and how you feel about it.

If you are furious and enraged about something, carve out a substantial block of time and write it out. Take a new yellow pad and fill the pages until you've detailed why you are mad and hurt, what happened, and who the dirty dogs are that did it to you.

Tactic six: Got a massager around your place? Millions of those things have been sold. We've got one we've had for years. I recently got it out after some strenuous activity had caused my feet to ache. Those things are great! Completely took my mind off of everything.

Tactic seven: Take a walk in the woods or a garden. There is some fascinating new research about the restorative power of nature on man. Almost every town, village and county in America has a park, a nature trail, a national forest, or a botanical garden. Most, if not free, are cheap. Talk a walk and concentrate on bird calls and animal tracks. Try to identify trees and leaves. A human remembers odors particularly efficiently. This is a skill rarely employed today outside of a handful of trades. Spending time concentrating on the odors of a forest is guaranteed to free your mind of the pressures of a search and leave you refreshed (even if a hike tires you out).

The Pep Talk

OK – here is the pep talk. Older people ARE getting hired.

From the *Wall Street Journal*:

> Aged to Perfection? More Companies Seek Older Leaders
>
> What does a corporate board of directors do when the chief executive isn't working out? Bring back an old leader who's, well, older.
>
> ….In the latest example, Boeing Co., Chairman and CEO Phil Condit resigned yesterday amid a string of scandals. Whom did the board tap to succeed him? Harry C. Stonecipher, Boeing's 67-year old retired president. And last week, Delta Air Lines Inc., mired in losses, picked outside board member Gerald Grinstein, **71**, to become CEO when Leo Mullins steps down Jan.1.
>
> …When New York Times Executive Editor Howell Raines resigned earlier this year in the wake of reporting scandals, the paper asked Joseph Lelyveld, 66, a former executive editor, to reassume the position temporarily….[20][21][22]

Don't give up. You too will find a position if you execute everything you've read to this point diligently and consistently. I'm sure it hasn't been fun so far, and it won't be fun until you've started that next position.

But be warned, after this brief pep talk, I'm going back to very tough, drill sergeant speak when you turn the page…

Chapter 25 The Next Job

"When you have to make a decision about someone's future, or what kind of weapons system to invest in, or any other kind of businesslike decision, you should not let anyone rush you." General Peter Pace, U.S. Marine Corp.

Yep soldier, that's what I said. In the new job battleground, the job search never stops. While accepting the new position, you must lay the ground work for finding the next one. In many lines of work, the average tenure is under four years, and trending towards three. Assume then that in three to four years, you will be doing this again! You're a veteran now, and understand the degree of difficulty. Now you must prepare the battleground to improve your odds of success the next time around, and to perhaps to even preempt the process by finding a new position before this one disappears.

The objective: For the remainder of your career, that you maintain high brand awareness, that is, maintaining the thousands of contacts that you've made. Make sure they know how to reach you, what you are doing, and how successful you are in your new role. Further, the quality of your communication and linkage to your contacts needs to be so high that your network continues to keep you informed about positions that they learn about, even though you are now employed.

Tactics: One, contact everyone that helped you and share the good news with them. I recommend that you make personal phone calls initially. For the numerous occasions that you get voice mail, leave the message that you've landed a new position; you are excited about it and please give you a call so you can tell them more. Since this is a good news call, and you aren't asking anyone to help; your response rate should be quite good.

Later on, follow-up with an email with all your new contact information, both work and home.

Update your social network. First, update LinkedIn. It will automatically notify everyone in your network. Then any others that you use: Spoke, Plaxo, Twitter, etc.

Finally, for search firm contacts, send them a letter with your new contact information a few weeks after the email.

This way, everyone gets contacted twice, and search firms three times. (Even with three contacts, many search firms won't get your new contact information right, so be prepared for that.)

Tactic Two: Join, join, join. As we covered in Chapter 11, every profession and every industry has professional and trade associations. And, do your public service. Churches, charities and the arts always need workers, contributors and financial supporters. Join, attend, and participate. (Now you know *first-hand* how important those contacts are, so cultivate them). And it will do your soul some good to give back a little.

Tactic Three: Continuous networking. Take time to call someone every day and email someone every day. That will be a minimum of 10 contacts per week. Assume that you attend two trade or professional meetings per month, making sure to speak to 10 people at each meeting, you will make 60 contacts per month, or 720 per year. *This is the minimum you need; recall that our target was to contact over 2,000 individuals.*

> *Insider tip one: at your professional and trade association meetings, do not talk and sit with the same group each month–maximize your contacts each meeting and cultivate an ever-expanding circle of relationships.*

Tactic Four: Reminders. I like to create reasons to send reminders. As the CFO of a public company, I mailed annual reports to a huge number of people with my card.

Tactic Five: Get published. There are virtually limitless opportunities in blogs, trade and professional periodicals to get your name in print. Leverage these and get the byline. Then, send reprints or URL links to the articles to your contacts. Follow both marketing guru Professor Kimberly Whitler and author and entrepreneur Guy Kawasaki on Twitter; they are geniuses at generating publicity. @KimWhitler; @GuyKawasaki.

Tactic Six: Start a blog. Keep it updated at least once per week. Send people a link so that they can follow what you are doing.